"STORIES INSPIRED BY KIDS WHO HAVE TOUCHED MY LIFE...AND CHANGED IT FOREVER."

VOICES IN THE HALL

TERRY PREUSS, NBCT

VOICES IN THE HALL By Terry Preuss

Front cover design courtesy of Thryth Navarro

Front cover photograph courtesy of © Matty Symons | Dreamstime.com

Editing and inspiration courtesy of Melanie Heywood

For more information, please visit www.terrypreuss.com

ABC+LOVE, Inc.

ISBN: 1463516541
ISBN 13: 9781463516543

ACKNOWLEDGEMENTS

Special thanks to my husband and sons for giving me the space and the freedom to give myself to these kids and this project.

To my parents, Albert and Mariana Lopez: thank you for teaching me to love. The best thing ever to happen to me was to be lucky enough to be born your daughter. Con tigo todo! Sin ti nada!.

To my brother and his wife, Joe and Thryth Navarro: my heartfelt thanks for believing in this work, and speeding it along!

To Melanie Heywood with whom writing has always been fun: here it is at last!

Grateful acknowledgement is made for permission to reproduce and/or narrate the journal entries of some of the students I taught, and which have been used throughout this book.

This book is based on real situations in kids' lives, and the journal entries written in their own words.

The names of students, locations, administrators, principals and schools quoted within have all been changed to protect their privacy, anonymity, and deniability.

The stories and characters may be composites of multiple individuals.

The stories may be dramatizations, and/or fictionalized versions of real events.

The views expressed in this work are solely those of the author.

ABC+LOVE, Inc.

A non-profit organization dedicated to bringing Brotherhood, Compassion and Love to every classroom and boardroom in America by educating educators and the public through troubled teens and at-risk youth, who become the adults of tomorrow.

(ABC+LOVE... It's About Brotherhood, Compassion+LOVE)
LOVE: Looking in Ourselves, Visioning Excellence in Education

This book is dedicated to, and inspired by, every student I have ever loved. For now they remain anonymous, but they know who they are. They loved me, trusted me, and taught me to love unconditionally and without judgment. They ring out a truth that many educational systems turn a blind eye to. For them I write these stories, so their voices can be heard…

I am your daughter. I am your son. I am your niece. I am your nephew. I am your grandchild. I am your student. I am your neighbor. I am that adolescent boy you see on a bike riding past you in traffic. I am the young girl walking next to you in the mall. I am a teenager in the twenty-first century.

THESE STORIES ARE INSPIRED BY KIDS WHO HAVE TOUCHED MY LIFE… AND CHANGED IT FOREVER.

I lie awake at night thinking of them, those kids who have opened up their hearts to me and who are in my care. I toss and turn, sweating their problems along with them. In my dreams...I think their thoughts. That's how well I know them. When I finally awaken it is always one of them I think of first.

I have my own children, but since I began teaching a self-contained Drop Out Prevention class, it's my students who first come into my mind upon awakening. Their troubled lives and their cries for help have woven themselves so deeply into my psyche that I can't seem to disconnect. They come to me even in my dreams...

PROLOGUE

DANIEL

DEAR WORLD,

My name is Daniel and my teacher wants to write a book to let parents know all about us kids. She wants you to know what our world is like. Listen to her cuz she knows. She teaches the toughest class in our school. She talks to us and she listens to us. We trust her and we tell her our stuff. She makes me feel like what we have to say is important, and like it would help you to know our feelings, so here goes.

Well, I think the first thing you need to know is that us kids need you to listen to us. Like when we come home, listen. Don't always be watching T.V. like you don't even care, and don't tell us to shut up when we try to say something. Then one day we don't even want to talk to you anymore. That's how it happened to me.

And now my parents are all like, "What's wrong with Danny?" Like whenever you go out and I'm by myself, you don't think of that. You just think of it when you want to. I had a lot of problems and nobody would help me. It was like I was invisible. Cuz all you do is work or do stuff you want to do. Even when you are in the house you are always doing your nails, or on the phone or watching T.V., or doing your bills. I thought you would talk to me when I got older, but you don't. I think you don't even really like me to be around. I think I just bother you. So I go to my room. Then if I'm too long in my room it's all like, "What's wrong? What are you doing locked in that room?" I don't get it. I don't understand what you want. Maybe if you told me I'd get it, but I don't. And I don't want to talk about it anymore.

But if I had to tell the world one thing, that's what I would tell them. You need to listen, and not just when you want to. You need to listen all the time, then maybe we wouldn't be hanging out with our friends who do drugs, and get into gangs and stuff like that.

LATOYA

DEAR WORLD,

I'm thirteen years old, and I started out just like most people, being cared for and loved. Even though I never knew my father, I had a mother's love, and that was enough. When I was five, my mother got a new boyfriend. He helped a lot with the bills, and I was happy for a while that I could call somebody "Daddy." When I was six my new, and first ever daddy, came into my room at night. He got in the bed with me. Held me. Made me feel safe. Kissed my forehead, rubbed my shoulders. Next day, he got me a doll. That's how it started. Months of that and feeling good and feeling loved.

Things started to change, and he started doing things that didn't feel good, and he started putting his hands on places where they shouldn't be. He would whisper in my ear, "It's okay, your mommy knows. She said we can do this." I believed him, so I never told my mom I didn't like it, but in my head, every night all I could think was, *please stop! I don't like it.*

I really believed him when he told me my mother knew. But some of the things he did to me felt wrong.

Sometimes I cried and yelled and he put his hand over my mouth. And he whispered in my ear, "I didn't mean to hurt you. Remember your mom said we could." He kissed my forehead and held me soft like he always did. "This will be our secret thing. You are a big girl now."

Later I cried, and he left before I stopped crying. Two days later it was the same thing. For four years this went on. It wasn't until after he left us that I understood how wrong it had been, what he'd done to me.

Being molested by a man who I called "Daddy" was the most painful experience of my life. He tricked me and he lied to me and I never knew until I was twelve years old that my mother hadn't told him it was okay for him to do those things. He made me really believe him, and even though something felt wrong, I trusted him. I let him, I never told, and now I feel like I was the stupidest person in the world. I feel used. I feel like I never got to have a childhood. He stole that from me and I'll never get it back.

HAILEY

DEAR WORLD,

I got into some heavy stuff a few months ago. I was babysitting for this couple and they always were taking ecstasy and they would give it to me. I would get so messed up. My mom, she liked them, so she let me go over all the time cuz they seemed like they were straight, but they were users, big time, and they sold too. I don't much know what they sold, but I know they did ecstasy all the time, so they had to sell that, but I think they sold coke too, and maybe crack. At least they had that around too, but it was the ecstasy they gave me, and I loved it so much I took it all the time.

I was so wasted one time in the car. A cop pulled us over and we were on our way to Key West, and Jerry rolled down the window and talked to him. I thought for sure we were busted. I had the babies in the back and the little one was crying, and I thought, *OMG!! I'm going to jail!* But all we got was a ticket. Then Jerry and Cindy were laughing and saying that having kids around makes them look so innocent. And they laughed their heads off all the way to freakin' Key West.

I was feeling great and my skin tingled and the wind was blowing in my hair on my cheeks. I was so high. I loved being high. I looked at the clouds. That one looked like a lion. Wow! It seemed like forever as we crossed over the ocean on the highway to the Keys.

I rolled a blunt for them in the backseat, and Jerry got pissed at me 'cause the baby grabbed it and all the weed fell, so Cindy had to give me more. She can't roll that good, so I have to do it. Then after we smoked the blunt I was so totally wasted, I don't remember getting there or anything. But once we were there in this crappy hotel, they kept giving me ecstasy all the time. A couple of times I forgot to change the babies and the big one, Nina, got a bad diaper rash, and cried the whole trip, and Jerry hit me on my face, and Cindy hit him for that, then they were fighting and throwing stuff all over the place and yelling. The next day we left.

DAWN

DEAR WORLD,

You know what I want is a good meal with lots of people sitting around a big table like when I lived in Missouri. Then my mom and dad got divorced and my mom brought me to Florida. I live in a low-life motel now and my mom is back drinking again. She had stopped for a long time, but she's back now and I know she's gonna die from it. They already told her she would die cuz of her liver, but she started drinking here in Florida.

I hate it when she drinks. I wish she would stop. Why can't she just stop? Who's going to take care of me if she really does die? Does she ever think about that? She don't care that I don't have nobody else!

We had an apartment first, but she couldn't pay and they kicked us out, and now we're at the Sand and Sea Motel on Pill Mill Highway. There are prostitutes here. I don't like it. I want to go back to Missouri. I bet I could live with my grandma or somebody that would cook for me. I'm eating at Mickey Dee's. That's my nick name for McDonald's. It's okay for a while, but I hate it now. Plus I had to do a grab and run before I paid and the one close to me don't want me back. But I didn't have any money and I wanted to eat. So now I have to take the bus to go to another McDonald's further away where they don't know I steal food.

My brother stayed with my Dad, and he wants to come here cuz my Dad is too strict and doesn't let him do nothing, but I tell him not to come. I hate riding buses all the time. It sucks. And my brother is littler than me so he won't be able to ride on so many buses like I do. He'll be stuck at home all day and there's big traffic on our street and there's nowhere to run or play. He would hate it even if he thinks it's better than staying with Dad. It's so way worse.

At least he gets along with his dad. I never did. He never liked me. He was always my dad, but not my real dad cuz my real dad died in a car accident when I was a baby. He was drunk driving when he died. People like that shouldn't drive. That's why we take buses here in Florida so my Mom won't have to drive no more cuz she don't have a driver's license.

DANIEL

The other day I got high for the first time. Everybody was laughing and having a good time at Trees Head Park where everybody hangs out after school. We were on the swings and Manny kept saying I should smoke, that it was a trip, and I'd love it, so I did it. It was freaky. I was laughing too and everybody was telling me I was really funny when I get high. I don't think I'll do it again though cuz I lost track of the time and when I got home it was late and my mom was asking all these questions and I didn't want to answer any of them.

LATOYA

I keep thinking about how things could be different if I could just shut out the bad thoughts, but they keep coming. I can't close them off and they bother me. Sometimes they just come when I don't expect them and I can't stop thinking about what my mom's boyfriend did, and how he lied and how I believed him and how stupid I was, and how I can't take it back or erase it, and then I'm sitting in class and somebody talks to me or says something fresh and I just explode. Then I get in trouble like when I have fights and stuff.

HAILEY

So when we got back from Key West, Jerry was still mad at me, but he asked me not to tell my mom he hit me so I could baby-sit some more. I told him okay, I wouldn't tell. They asked my mom if I could live with them and she said okay since she got a new boyfriend and our place is too small for all three of us. So I got some stuff and lived with Jerry and Cindy for a whole summer. Their house is big and has a yard. I took ecstasy all summer until Jerry tried to get me to get in bed and have sex with Cindy. That's messed up cause I just don't get into none of that lesbian, girl on girl stuff. I know boys like it these days and a lot of girls think it's cool and stuff, but that's not me. Nope. I don't do nothing like that. If you don't like girls why r u gonna kiss them and make like you do, so some boy likes you? So I stopped babysitting. I think that's why they were giving me the ecstasy all the time. They're probably into that three way stuff. Even kids are getting into that, but not me. It's plain stupid. I don't like touching on no girls cuz they are soft and mushy feeling and no amount of ecstasy will change that.

DAWN

Last night one of the prostitutes had a guy in the room right by us. I kept trying to hear, but they were quiet. The owner doesn't like the prostitutes around, but sometimes they sneak in cuz someone else rents a room for them so he doesn't know who it's for, but I see at night cause they stand right on the street in front and try to get guys to take them around. They get in the cars with them and they park out back, and sometimes they come in one of the rooms. I always act like I don't know what's going on and they think since I'm a kid I'm stupid and stuff. But I know exactly what's going down. That's why I hate it here.

Mom says we're going to move out when she gets enough money, but she hasn't been able to go to work cuz she's so sick in the morning. She's going to find a job where she works at night.

DANIEL

Can't you even tell when I'm high? I can be wasted and you don't even know. I got home and you were pissed at me for being late, but you didn't know I was high. I guess you would never think I would do it. If I do it again, I wonder if you'll notice. Probably not. You are too involved with my little brothers to notice me anyway. I think you love them more than me since you are married to their father. Sometimes I just feel like I'm in the way.

LATOYA

When he left us, I finally told my mom the truth. We tried to sue him, but he had left the state, and they said it was my word against his, and that I waited too long to tell. But when I found out he had given me syphilis we thought we could really get him, that if he had it too, the courts would have to listen to me. Then one day my Mom let him come over when he was in town to visit her, and just because of that the court said I had no case because my mom thought he was safe enough to let him visit. So he's living in Chicago now and we never could do anything or put him in jail where he belongs. I'll never understand why grown-ups can hurt kids like that and keep living. So many times I just want to die.

I want to stop the thoughts, but the thoughts keep coming.

And sometimes I'm just sitting in school thinking about this and the teacher asks me a question and then just yells at me for not listening. I don't mean to not listen. My head just goes places. That's how come I failed so many classes.

HAILEY

I had some ecstasy in my purse when I went back to my mom's and I told her what happened and she was pissed. But I didn't tell her everything, just the part that Cindy gave me ecstasy and wanted me to have sex and she laughed, and told me not to hang around with them anymore. I showed her the ecstasy and she got high with me. I had never gotten high with my mother before. My Mom is so cool! She said it was okay cuz I was with her, but she said she didn't want me getting high by myself. She would freak if she knew how messed up I got everyday with Jerry and Cindy.

DAWN

My mom can be so mean when she's drunk. Last night she said she wished she never had me and that I was slowing her down. She said she hated me. She said she doesn't want to see me for a few days.

Moms aren't supposed to say stuff like that to their kids. Why does she say she hates me? Do you mean it or is it just cuz you're drunk? You are supposed to love me. Why can't you be nice to me like other Moms? You were nice in Missouri. I just don't get it.

I'm going to stay with my friend Dalia for a while. She has a boyfriend who is older and he has an apartment and it's cool if I crash there, plus we can take the bus to school together and stuff. I know my mom. If I go away for a few days then she'll be sorry for what she said.

DANIEL

If you would just pay attention to me it could be like we're a family. I know he's just my stepdad, but I can't even remember my own dad, he's in jail for life, so as far as I'm concerned he is my dad. I don't think he loves me like his own sons.

LATOYA

How could my mom not know what he was doing? How could I have been so stupid and let him do that to me? Why wasn't anyone listening at night? Isn't home the one place you are supposed to be safe?

HAILEY

I have the coolest mom ever! I really love that I can get high with her and she is like okay with stuff. She's always there for me. I'm really lucky.

DAWN

Why does my mom care more about drinking than she cares about me?

CHAPTER ONE - YEAR ONE

THE BEGINNING

I am so fortunate to be the benefactor, the observer, and the one person who gets to watch, hear, and listen to kids like Danny, Latoya, Hailey, and Dawn. No amount of *Newsweek* or *Time* articles or *Parent's* magazines prepared me for this: for the attack on my senses that leaves me breathless at times; tired, worn out, worried, and in tears, even on a good day. These stories are about my charges, over whom I have little stewardship, and yet I have infinite compassion for and whom I love and care. In the end, my classroom is a microcosm of society, and my students are the emblems of what ails and what inspires.

My classroom is filled with students at risk in the Alternative Education *Drop Out Prevention Program* (DOP) within Sunshine County Public Schools. My DOP students have been labeled as: *"difficult, unmanageable, troubled kids, who sometimes have criminal records, and care very little about school."* Some of them have been in and out of jail numerous times, many of them have little support at home, all of them failed last year and have recurrent conduct referrals, and most of them can look a little scary and mean. For many of them, my class is their last chance to succeed in school.

Their stories are painful at times, but it's important that we understand what kids are living through today. I want to share what they have brought to my life, but before I go on, let me tell you how it all began.

I've been a professional educator for the last fifteen years; first in Physical Education, then in Language Arts. It was just two years ago that I left Beach County Public Schools in the Miami area, and decided to work closer to home. I was fortunate to find work immediately with Sunshine County Schools, which is a bit further north and covers more of Boca/ Fort Lauderdale and surrounding areas.

When I interviewed for this job, the principal offered me two possible positions. One would be a traditional Language Arts position teaching six periods a day. The other she said wasn't for everyone, so of course it piqued my interest. "It's called *'DOP'*— that stands for *Drop Out Prevention*. I need someone really strong to go in there and keep these kids in line. They've chased out two teachers already."

I looked at her, all confidence and smiles. As a substitute teacher in California, I had spent most of my time in Alternative Education schools, which most subs avoided like the plague. I had taught Language Arts in a similar program in Beach County. There it was called *SARP: Students At Risk Program*. "They won't chase me out. I'm not worried about that."

"Well, there's more. We do it differently at this school. It's a self-contained classroom," she said. I looked at her blankly, but said nothing.

I really didn't know what in the world that meant. Coming from a background of Physical Education, and never having taught elementary school, it was a term I was completely unfamiliar with. Fortunately, she went on so I didn't have to reveal my ignorance.

"You'll have to teach them all their subjects, and you'll be with the same kids all day long. They're a tough bunch. They've all failed at least once, some of them multiple times. They'll be in seventh grade until January, and if you pass them they'll be transitioned to the eighth grade. They do two years in one, but they'll stay with you till June. The ages will range from twelve to sixteen in one classroom and behavior problems are usually rampant."

She paused. "Some will have criminal records." She looked up over her glasses to see if she had lost me, and then smiled. "I keep the DOP classes small, so you'll never have more than 28 kids."

That hooked me. In Miami, my Language Arts classes had gotten as high as 42 students at times, and Physical Education could go up over to over 80 for one teacher in some schools. I'd not only worked with difficult students before, but had worked with them in much higher numbers, and rather enjoyed them. The only part that worried me was the "be-with-the-same-kids-all-day-and-teach-them-all-their-subjects" part. I'd never done that, and I suddenly got a tinge of math anxiety creeping up on me—something I've suffered from since the second grade, when Mrs. Williams would send me out of her room with math problems as punishment for talking in her class.

"None of that worries me," I said, trying to look confident. "I don't think I would mind being with the same kids all day. I'm known for being good with discipline, and I tend to connect well with the type of student you are describing. Actually, it sounds like an interesting challenge, but I do have one problem." She looked at me seriously. "I don't think I can teach math. It's like I'm dyslexic with numbers." *Why did you say that? She's going to think you're an idiot!*

She looked at me and smiled. "If you're not worried about the discipline, I'm certain you'll find a way to handle the math." She stood up, shook my hand. The job was mine! *Whew!*

I really didn't worry much about anything for the several weeks that followed. I took all of the books home and started planning lessons in Geography and Science, and yes, even Math. I'd never taught any of those subjects before. It was like I was a new teacher all over again. It was all quite exhilarating. I was ready to rumble when August 22, that first year, rolled in and I had to show up for my first teacher-planning day. That's when the trouble started.

Every teacher who met me came to sympathize with the difficult task I was undertaking. I heard all about the teachers these *"terrible"* kids had *"run out."* One of them just left campus in the middle of the day never to return. Another one had been a correctional officer in an adult detention center, and hadn't lasted either. I went to my room to try to organize my materials, but frankly, I was beginning to get worried. Could these kids be that much worse than the kids in Miami? *What had I gotten myself into? Who am I kidding? What am I going to do with the same kids all day long? My classroom will be an infernal prison, and the hostage will be me!*

I don't think I slept at all the night before school started and I began to have second thoughts about the change. I mean, what was I thinking? I changed counties just to save myself from twenty minutes of traffic in the morning. I loved my previous school. I loved my previous boss. I had been happy enough. *Why did I do this? Those kids are going to eat me alive!!*

When they walked in to my room the next morning, I held my head high, pretending to be in complete control of my environment. I had brought in several unique and boldly-colored art furniture items from my husband's art gallery that I thought would make a good impression on the kids and make the otherwise stale classroom more inviting. Several of the twenty-seven students on my roll sheet were absent. I had a room full of boys. Not one girl.

They looked around at the unusual desks and colorful furniture, and they seemed to like it. Some of them looked a bit mean and maybe even a little scary, and sure, a few tried to act smart, but I started in with my first-day-of-school-and-I'm-the-boss-so-don't-even-try-it-routine, and they fell right into place with surprising ease.

I looked around the room at a motley crew of boys all staring back at me, listening, doing what I said, and appearing to be interested and attentive. I knew then that it was going to be okay. What I didn't know is that I would soon develop an incredible bond with this class of kids who had been labeled "*difficult, troubled, behavior problems.*" I didn't know that I would get to know each and every one of them and their families on such an intimate level, or that I would feel compelled to write a book about my experience.

I only knew that they weren't going to run *me* out—not on the first day anyway. I knew I could handle them. I knew I wanted to succeed. I knew that because it was "alternative education," I could do things a little differently. So from day one, I built time into the curriculum for "*listening and caring.*" I mean, I had the same kids all day, so I was in no hurry, and

I instinctively sensed that they needed to share, and wanted desperately to have someone listen to them. So after we got all the first-day-of-school business out of the way, and I familiarized them with the books and the curriculum, we ended the day by getting in a circle and talking about ourselves.

We discussed a lot of things, but mostly how they felt about having failed and being in a DOP class, and what we did over the summer. Then we wrote about it. Then some of us shared our work. I was just another one of the participants. That's how it all started.

I really didn't know what else to do to get to know them, and I knew I'd have to get to know them if we were going to be spending the whole day together, every weekday for the next ten months. Through the talking and the writing we opened up a whole world of communication, and later it became our standard first period assignment. It's how we started every day. I'd write a journal topic on the board and we'd write about it, or some days we'd just talk about it. Usually it was an interdisciplinary topic found within the curriculum, but other days it was about something that had happened in class, or in the world.

I found my students to be the most fascinating individuals I'd ever come across. Their stories were so wild, wonderful, hilarious, and painful. They told remarkable tales of what their lives were like and how they felt about living. Sometimes I'd have to stop them because I'd be in tears, or I didn't want to hear anymore because some things they talked about were illegal. Some of their stories were so poignant they reminded me of Nietzsche's admonition— to be careful when you look into the abyss because sometimes it looks back at you.

I realized that although I'd been doing this writing and sharing activity for years as a Language Arts teacher, now it was different. I had these kids all day. I knew them intimately.

I didn't have to worry about a bell ringing and all of them having to go to their next class. We could really get into topics that were important and relevant. I wasn't rushed.

I had, for the first time in my career, enough time to fully develop my lessons, discuss them in ways the kids understood and could relate to, then create cognitive activities they enjoyed. Sometimes we would spend half a day on one lesson. It was wonderful!

They were learning and expressing themselves, and opening up in surprising and unexpected ways about the way they live and the way they saw others live. I let them talk things through. I let them express their opinions. I let them use their own experiences as a point of reference to better construct learning pathways on the various topics within the curriculum. We developed a comfortable and relaxed learning environment. We became a family.

After a while I told them, "Guys, I'm going to have to write a book about this. People need to know how kids think and live today." They were all very supportive, and so were their families. They trusted me to tell their stories, and publish some of their work. But as my vision for this book began to solidify, I realized they'd done more than that. They had reconnected me, in remarkably insightful ways, with all the other stories of all the other students who I'd been involved with over the course of my tenure as an educator.

Even though many of these students encouraged me to use their real names in connection with their actual stories, I told them I would prefer to keep their anonymity. In this way, their voices could become mingled with thousands of other voices I'd heard before, all shouting forth a powerful message that begged to be told.

I hope I can honor those first kids who inspired this book to come forth. They are the ones who changed me forever. They were the first and most pivotal force behind this work.

But their lives and their stories are now merged with others, sometimes creating composites or collective personas that represent what we are facing today in every classroom across America. And while all the bureaucrats and educators scurry around trying to find answers and solutions to the problems with education, these kids have taught me that we are neglecting to look the problems squarely in the eye. Their eyes.

Since then, another self-contained DOP class has crossed my path. They too are touching me and teaching me, and connecting me even further with the universal voice of today's troubled youth. They have joined with the others I've taught, and known. They too join thousands of voices that have touched me in such profound ways that their stories have woven themselves into the fabric of my being. I can never again disconnect myself from the problems they are facing as I attempt to teach them. I have come to understand that the problems they face as a community of youth are the very reason it's difficult to teach so many of them. I can't ignore how they live, or the struggles their young lives face, day in and day out.

As you read, remember, I am merely the purveyor of the message. The message is what these kids have to say. What they speak. What they write. How they show up each day. What they want you to know. What they have communicated with me throughout my years of service to them. They beckoned a voice with which to reach you. I will be that voice. They speak through me. If you listen carefully, perhaps you too will find something that deeply resonates. If at times your heart aches, and at other times it races, that is when you are there with me and with them in the classroom. So please listen when they speak, as they alone hold the answers to what ails them, education, and society. Sit back, relax, and learn what you can from the *Voices in the Hall.*

THE BOYS

DANIEL

When I walked in the room, I thought what the heck is going on in here? There are orange cow spots around the chalkboard, and a chair that looks like Marilyn Monroe and you can sit on its lap, and a big purple couch, and a comfortable recliner, and a rad looking rocking chair. The teacher lets us sit in the rocking chair and talk about stuff. I asked why the room looked so wack. She said we had to be here all day, so she wanted to make the room look more fun and she said she wanted us to have comfortable places to sit and think and learn. That's straight up. Maybe this class won't be so bad after all.

CARLOS

Today we just looked at all the books we're going to use, and the teacher let us pick what chapters we wanted to cover first. No one has ever let me pick stuff before. I think maybe this class is gonna be str8, but it's too early to tell. Some of these teachers can throw on the charm in the first few days, then later their true colors come out. Not to say that's gonna happen to you. My mom has cancer, so sometimes my mind drifts, and maybe you'll notice I start to cry. If that happens will you let me go outside?

RIVO

I think this class is going to be okay. The teacher was letting us talk about ourselves and I liked that. Like I got to hear about what everybody did this summer and we were laughing and having fun, but she was teaching us stuff at the same time. And when I told everybody about how I got in trouble for stealing, she was cool with it. She let me talk. Then she said we'd be writing in these journals every day, and she said she didn't count off for bad spelling. That's cool cause I don't spell so good. So tomorrow we can share these if we want to. But I'm not going to cause I don't have that much to say.

TONY

My new teacher's name is Mrs. Preuss. She says, it sounds like "*Rolls Royce*." Today some kids gave her a hard time, but she handled it. She seems to like us, which is a first around here. Last year I was in this class, in this same room, actually. That teacher hated us. I never would come, so of cause, I failed again. Needless to say, I'm not too happy about that.

N-E ways, Teach, I want you to know I like what you did with the room, especially the "Share if you Dare Chair." And for the record, I'm not stupid like some of the other kids who fail the seventh grade. I have like a 180 IQ. I just don't like school, and even if I fail again it won't matter because as soon as I'm sixteen I can legally drop out. So one way or another, this year may be the one. Either I'll pass, or I'll just turn sixteen and stop coming. One thing is for sure, I won't be doing the seventh grade a fourth time.

You seem reasonable, so I guess I'll show up tomorrow.

RANDY

I done the 7th grade three times so I should be like in 11th grade. I made myself a promise I'm gonna do it this time, but I can't see how I can wake up and sh** everyday and get here by 7 am. It's gonna be hard. But I don't want to be one of those drop-out low lives with only a 7th grade education. I wanna at least be able to say I been to high school.

ARMANDO

I like to write in journals. My teacher last year did that, but she graded them. You said you don't grade them for spelling and stuff, only if we wrote a whole page then we would get an A. I'll try to fill up a page. I want to pass this year. Tomorrow I'll write more.

PETER

I was sad when they told me I was going to be in the DOP class, cause last year me and my friends always called the DOP class, "Dumb on Purpose" and we would make fun of them all the time. Today the DOP teacher said in her class DOP means "Doing Our Personal-Best." She says all we have to do is the best we can and we'll pass. Usually I do the best I can, but I failed anyway, and in 5th grade too. If it's true what she says then I'll pass, cause I do my best most times. But I don't know, I'm probably gonna fail again. I guess I never should have made fun of DOP.

NIKOLAS

Summer was a pain in the a**. I had to move from New York and leave all my friends. My mom and dad split up, but my dad won't leave her alone, so my mom had to leave the whole state. She says the cops don't do sh** till somebody's dead. I had to help her pack up everything. My big brother is staying there. I love my big brother. I love my dad too, but my mom said I had to come here to f*** a** Florida. Nothing's good about being here. Nothing.

KIKO

My teacher told me I could swear in these journals if I had to. She said it's not like other writing. She said to just write my feelings, and write like I talk. Okay, so I'll try to do that. She says if we know how to talk then we know how to write. She wrote on the board, "Talking… Is Writing… Is Reading!" I never thought of it like that. But I'll write a lot if I don't have to worry about spelling and grammar and stuff like that.

RAFE

This summer I got high every day. I got totally wasted. I had a blast. That concludes my journal.

KYLE

This summer I played my guitar and wrote songs. I'm going to be a musician. I like heavy metal, and I like going to mosh pits. As far as this class goes, just stay out of my way and we'll be fine.

BOBBY

I had a great summer with my family. I wish I hadn't of failed, but now I'm here and I can do two years in one. I want to make my mom happy again, so I'm going to try to pass this class.

Today I told everybody about how good of a skateboarder I am, and how I was skateboarding around all summer long at Brian Piccolo Park. And I even got in the middle of the room and showed how my favorite tricks work. Everybody was laughing. I like it when everybody laughs.

CHUNGO

I'm fourteen years old, and I failed last year, but this year I'm going to do good. I'm trying to put the past behind me and forget what I've seen. I block out the memories of my uncle dying in front of me. I block out the gunshots outside my window, and watching two people die in front of me. I'm gonna try to keep my mind on my schoolwork, but sometimes it's hard. I'm going to get a good grade now. I'm in a special class. I want to make my parents proud. I want to prove I can do it, but the memories take over sometimes.

DILLON

I'm skeptical about being here in this class with all these DOP Dopes. I don't belong here. The only reason I failed last year is because I missed a lot of school because my parents moved after their divorce, and some of my teachers failed me on the last quarter because of bad attendance. I'm not like these criminal types in here. Can I please go see a counselor and try to get out of your class? I mean, nothing personal, but I don't belong here. These are bad kids. I'm not a bad kid.

TREYVOHN

One thing I can say is that if we don't get some girls in this class, I'm outta here. I don't just wanna look at these bum ugly faces all day. I know a lot of these people from last year, and some of them I hate. Like buddy over there staring me down all the time like he wants to start sh**. I don't want no trouble, so I better get some females in here to get my mind off all the unfinished business from last year. I still gotz a few heads to bash here and there and a few of them are sitting right here in this room.

GHOST

This summer I got a record for breaking and entering. I just got out of jail. Jail sucks. No way I'm going back there again. About this DOP class, I'm always in DOP. Don't know nothin' else, so for me it's just the usual, except usually nobody ever asks me so many questions like this. And by the way, I know you saw my ankle bracelet, but you played it off like you didn't. That was real decent of you. Yeah, I'm on house arrest, but I am allowed to come to school. I don't wanna go back to jail, so I have to do good and I can't get into no fights. I hope all these jits I see here leave me alone and don't try starting no trouble.

JUAN

I just moved here from New Jersey. I have to live with my older brother now cause my mom says she can't stand me no more. So she's in New Jersey with my sister, and I'm here. My brother is strict and he says I can't pull none of the sh** I used to pull with my mother.

I'm not so good at writing. I'm not good at spelling. I think I'm gonna fail again. I don't like to do my work. It's boring.

ROLANDO

This summer I came close to killing this guy. I was so mad at him cause he said some sh** about my girlfriend, and my friend said he could get me a gun, but my girl said don't do it. So I didn't. I failed last year cause I didn't come to school, and I'll probably fail this year too cuz I don't usually come.

RAMON

I had to take care of my father this summer. He's in a wheelchair, and my mom walked out on him so he doesn't have anybody to take care of him. My auntie is usually there, but she went on vacation this summer, so I had to stay in and help him.

I only failed because my science teacher hated me. That's the reason. Then I didn't come to summer school, so now I'm f***ed!

ALEX

You want to know about my summer? Well it sucked cuz I found out that my mother is a no good b****. I went to see her in Kansas City and she didn't even give a damn. She acted like she was going to do stuff with me and then she hardly came by and I was two weeks just with my grandmother.

TREVOR

I failed because I fooled around a lot last year then they said I had to go to summer school. I came, but I fooled around in summer school too. I have a lot of friends in this class, so it'll be all right. We all fooled around together last year, and now we're here together. This is going to be fun.

THE GIRLS

More than three weeks went by before a girl walked through my door. When Ashley first stepped foot into my room, there were only boys officially registered in my class: big, mean and hairy ones; squirrelly ones; wiry ones; fat ones; Casanova wannabes; smart ones; learning-disabled; hot-looking; slick ones; shy ones; quiet ones; comedians; nerdy ones; cool ones; scary ones; lovable ones; happy ones; depressed ones. Everything, in every color, was sitting in that room.

Ashley came in all soft and smelling sweet with golden hair and green eyes. Her face was perfect: chiseled nose, pouty lips, rosy cheeks. She looked like a model, tall and slender, all legs and not an ounce of fat. I could almost smell the testosterone levels rise as she sashayed over to my desk in her very tight jeans.

I explained to her that she was the only girl, and I asked her if she would mind that. She looked around the room, then looked in my eyes assuring, "I'll be all right."

She looked like she'd been around the block. I could smell a trace of cigarettes mingled with her cologne. Her green eyes looked like they'd seen quite a bit in their young experience, but they twinkled. I liked her immediately, and when she took a seat and I started teaching, a wonderful thing happened.

She watched my every move. She absolutely hung on to every word I said. She took notes, and she kept an organized folder. Every day was just like that. She was always attentive, always following along with the lesson. She tried to always do her homework, and she listened to everything I said. It wasn't just that she was attentive; it was the way she looked at me. It was as if she was studying every move I made. She was transfixed, absorbing every word. Not only that, if anyone in the class talked out of turn, she would shut them up.

"I'm trying to listen. What's the matter with you? Have some respect. Are you some kinda idiot?" she'd shout out, turning her head in the direction of the unsolicited comments. She often looked ready to back her words up with a fist down someone's throat. I must say, at times I was taken aback.

She wielded so much power as the only female for a few weeks. With Ashley around, keeping discipline became less of a chore. One thing was for sure, she was determined to pass my class. She wanted to do everything just as I requested it. That's how our story began.

In time, I would become very close to her. Things would happen in her life that would change me forever. She would often tell me that she loved me, and I would say, "I love being loved by you!" I meant it, too. It's a pleasure to teach when you have someone in your class who loves you that much.

After Ashley, other girls soon came. But they would remain the small minority for the entire year. The first to come after Ashley was a beautiful black girl called Latoya. Her smile lit up an entire room, and she would come to gain a place in my heart that will be hers forever. She and Ashley became fast friends for a few days, but then they were enemies for most of the year; often fighting, drawing blood, and insulting each other in loud and astounding ways. I could never turn my back on the room, for fear they would go at each other.

Most of the year, on any given day, only two to four girls would show up for class. They came and went. Most of the others enrolled late and withdrew early in the year, but there were several and they left a lasting impact.

ASHLEY

I've lived a lot of places like South Carolina and New York. I'm happy now cuz I'm living here with my mom. I miss my little brother and I think of him all the time, but I can't live with my dad no more cuz he was hitting me, so I'm here now and me and my mom are gonna be all right in sunny South Florida.

LATOYA

I'm here in this class because I failed and didn't come to summer school. I don't want to fail again, so I'll do everything you say. I promise to be your best student. I don't want to let myself and my family down again. I want to work with children when I grow up, so I need an education. I want to get good grades, and I want to go to a good University. Maybe I'll go to a famous black University like my auntie. I want to become a Pediatrician, you know, a doctor for kids.

DAWN

I'm gonna tell you a little about myself, okay. But mostly my life sucks because my mom is an alcoholic, and my dad is dead. When I was born I was only two pounds and nobody thought I would live, but here I am, so it's all good..

DALIA

I am going to be okay in this class because here everybody is like me. At my school before, I always the oldest one, but in this class everybody is like me. Here everybody failed. I like that I will write a lot and learn better my English.

HAILEY

I'm not so good at school but I'm trying to get my life together. I should be in high school already. If I can do two years this year, then I will only be one year behind, and I can say I made it to high school. That would be great and I will be so thankful if this can happen to my life. I do take drugs, but I won't take them when I come to school. I promise!

RAINEY

This class has a lot of fine a** boys and hip as sh** girls up in here. That's very cool because I've never been popular and I'm not good at making friends or meeting guys. But if I'm here with all these cool people, I think I'll be friends with them, then maybe I'll be cool too.

SA'RINA

I've had some sad moments this summer because my mother left to Colorado and I moved in with my dad. Because of this my family will not speak to me, but I don't know why I should have to be the one to go with my mother and leave all my friends, and my school. Besides I found out my mother takes pills. She had a whole drawer with pills of all different colors. All the upheaval caused me to get depressed and fail last quarter, after always having been a good student, so they put me in your class.

Now my mom is saying my dad is not a good person and that I should leave and go to Colorado, but I'll never believe what they say about my dad, what they say he did, that he molested my neighbor. I just won't ever believe it and I just know my mother is making it all up, her pill taking self.

TAKESHA

I wish I was at Kewl Middle School where them cute boys stay at. But they made me come to Destiny. Some boys here are cute, but I wanted to be at Kewl. My homegurlz go there.

SOPHIA

I'm not sure I can come to school every day. The courts made me come cuz I haven't come in two years. I'm supposed to be in the tenth grade, not in the seventh. And I hate school, and my boyfriend doesn't want me to come, but they told my mom she would go to jail if I didn't come, so here I am. I mostly live with my boyfriend, not my mom, so I don't know why it's her place to get me over here anyway. She never wanted me when she had me, and it's no different now. But I don't want her to go to jail, so I have to come, I guess. Even though she's been to jail plenty of times, just overnight, you know, for when she turns tricks. They know her there, and she gets right out. But I think if your kids don't go to school then they keep you in there longer, so here I am, so my mom stays out of trouble.

SANDRA

I just want to say thank you for letting me be in your class even though I'm pregnant. I know you could have said no, but you let me stay, so thank you. I really want to finish my education and I know I made some mistakes, but this baby is because somebody raped me, so it ain't my fault. Do you believe me?

CHAPTER TWO

KYLE

Kyle came into my room the first day of school wearing a demonic t-shirt, and acting up. He was trying to call attention to himself, acting like a real "bad boy." He would ask questions and make comments geared at totally derailing my attempts to give the rest of my class an education. Finally, halfway through the second period on the first day of class, I got tired of his infantile attempts to test my limits, and I called him outside for a private talk.

I got him just outside the door, pointed inside and said, "That nonsense you're pulling in there isn't gonna fly with me."

He just looked at me. No expression. So I went on.

"You want attention don't you? Well, you can't have it at my expense. I've given you almost two hours to get a grip, and it hasn't worked." Still nothing. Just a stare, so I got closer.

"I don't want to embarrass you in front of the entire class, but I will if I have to. Do you get my meaning?" I said that in my scariest teacher voice, looking right in his eyes, hoping, of course, to scare him a little bit. It didn't seem to be working. So, I softened up.

I threw some God-honest compassion into my voice, and stepped back to give him some breathing room. "Now, if there's something you want to say to me, say it now." I searched deeper into his black, fiery eyes. "Is there something bothering you? Is there anything I can help you with?"

He looked down, seemingly embarrassed by my humanity…

"Because if you need to talk to me one on one, I'm all into that. But you're going to have to act like a gentleman in my room if we're going to get along."

I figured he understood I was willing to meet him halfway by this point, so I thought it was time to lay down the facts as I saw them, even though his neck was spinning around so far he looked like Gumby.

"If you don't want to get along with me, that's your choice," I said into the back of his head with its very black, very short, very curly hair. "But I can tell you, it's going to be a long and miserable year for both of us, seeing as how we're going to be holed up in that room six hours a day... together...all year long."

I tapped on his shoulder. "Hey, I'm over here." He finally turned around and looked at me.

"So what's it gonna be? Can I help you get a grip somehow, or are we gonna go to battle in there? Cause I'll tell you right now, if you want to battle, I'll win. Teachers always do." I stared at him, not flinching at his gaze. I thought he was beginning to get my meaning. "I think it's best if we get along, and respect each other. What do you say?"

Usually this kind of speech would soften most kids up, either they get a little scared, and they decide they'd better not mess with me, or they sense that I'm someone they can talk to and they soften up, and open up. Normally right about now the student says some wonderful thing, we shake hands and go back inside and play nice. You know what he said to me?

"I like to blow people up."

"What?"

"You know, dynamite, bombs. I like to blow people's heads off". He was looking at me with a macabre grin across his face.

"Really?" I stay outwardly cool, but the thoughts that were racing through my head were sobering.

"Yeah, last year we cleared the school out. Swat team came. That was me." He was laughing, grinning with pride.

"Sounds like you're really proud of yourself for interrupting everyone's education," I said. He just shrugged, so I continued.

"Have you ever actually blown anybody's head off?"

"No," he said and looked away.

"Well then, I guess I have nothing to worry about, cause I don't suspect you'll be blowing anyone's head off today. Now get yourself back in my room and sit like a gentleman and listen to my lesson."

"Man lady, you're wack," he said shaking his head.

"What'd you say?" I came real close to his face.

"Nothin'. Nothin.'"

"That's what I thought. 'Nothin' is the best thing for you to have said, and nothin' is what I'm planning to hear from you for the rest of the day. Now go in my room and play nice," I opened the door and he walked in and sat in his chair. The whole class was quiet, wondering what had been said outside. Kyle went in and sat down. He didn't interrupt me for the rest of that day.

Of course the first chance I got, I started a file on him, documenting his odd comments. I spoke with the counselor to find out about his past, and how seriously to take this bomb threat of his. Everyone told me he just did that to get attention, but I was cautious for many weeks.

After that, I fell in love with Kyle. He became one of my most important challenges. I was determined to get him to succeed in my class and pass on to high school, but there were a few hurdles to cross.

On the second day of school, he wore another satanic t-shirt. I noticed it immediately but said nothing. Later he started to draw pentagrams on his desk and book-bag. I mentioned it to him in front of the class.

"Interesting artwork," I said. "What's up with that?"

"He's a head banger, Mrs. Preuss, he thinks the Devil is cool," came a voice from across the room.

I'd never heard that term before. "Head banger?" I looked at Kyle. "So you think the Devil is cool, do you?"

"Yeah." He looked straight in my eyes for a minute before he went back to drawing his pentagrams.

We went back and forth for a few days about what it meant to be a head banger and why they used the Devil as a symbol. He seemed to like the attention, and clung to my apparent curiosity in his unusual interests. He liked to talk about all his head banger music, and he became very animated telling me about how he was going to be a heavy metal musician one day, but I'd had quite enough with the pentagrams and the demonic paraphernalia. Knowing I had to be careful about the student's right to freedom of speech and expression, I went to my administrator for advice on what I could do.

I knew that t-shirts with profanity, racist or offensive comments, cigarettes, alcohol or controlled substances were banned. But the Devil? I just wasn't sure about that.

"If it's offensive to you, Mrs. Preuss, it's offensive to your classroom," my administrator assured me. That was just the ammunition I needed.

About another week had gone by and Kyle was becoming a daily amusement, who along with his intermittent disruptions, also insulted my sensitivities with constant talk of the Devil, and flagrant demonic symbols for all to see. But at least I was no longer afraid that he would make good on his threats to blow people's heads off, at least not mine. I figured, what have I got to lose?

I took the opportunity one day when I was flaming mad at him over something he'd done to disrupt instruction. I went right over to his desk. He was drawing a pentagram on his forearm. I took the pen right out of his hand. He shot up and started acting tough. "Hey, you can't just take a pen out of my hand."

"I think I just did."

"Give it back."

"Nope." I walked over to my desk and threw the pen down in the center of it.

He went over like he wanted to grab it. "Don't even think about it," I said positioning myself between him and my desk.

"Man, Lady, that's my pen."

"Really? Well you never use it to do your work. In fact you don't much do any work at all. All I ever see you use it for is to make your little symbols all over the place, and I'm tired of your little symbols." I stood squarely in front of him. "Now, go sit down."

This could have really gone any number of ways and I was really quite surprised when Kyle went and sat down. So I figured I was on a roll. "Now that I have your attention, I have a few other things to say... I'm tired of you disrupting my class with all your constant foolishness, but I can see you're smart, so I don't want to lose you on that account, but I promise you this ... if you come into my room one more time with any of your Devil stuff *on*, *near* or *around* you, you're gone. I won't let you into my room. You got that?"

"I can wear whatever I want," he retorted defiantly.

"Not in my room you can't."

"I don't have any other clothes."

"Then I guess you'll have to go shopping," I said, "because I don't want to see any more sculls, skeletons, Devils or demons screaming off your shirts."

"You can't do that."

"It's offensive to me. I don't want to look at or think about dead things and demons all day, so if you plan to stay in this class, you'd better find yourself a new wardrobe. Otherwise, I'll march us right down to the office and see if they can put you back in regular classes."

Lo and behold, I never saw another one of those shirts again! He was still disruptive, but in an amusingly endearing way. Besides, he was a great writer and a good listener, always had answers to my questions, and his reading scores were some of the highest in the class. He was smart. He had a chance to make something of himself, and I wanted very much to help him make it. I worked extra hard to deal with his behavioral issues that were legendary in the school. There weren't many teachers who could stand the sight of Kyle sitting in their room. But, I grew to love him.

After months of doing well, with just the occasional and expected misbehaviors that were bound to circulate in the vicinity of Kyle, one day I was giving instruction to a perfectly quiet classroom, when I caught him receiving something from Sandy, the girl sitting next to him. I thought it was bubble gum.

Sandy was four months pregnant, but one of my top students. Kyle had an unusually guilty look on his face. I went up to him and held out my hand. He started to squirm. By this time a few months into our relationship, Kyle would have put a piece of gum or candy into my hand. I knew then it was something worse.

"Give it up," I said, motioning with my hand close to his face. He just froze. Sandy sunk about two inches. The whole class remained silent. I wondered what Sandy could have given him that he was so petrified to show me. They all know how I feel about gum. But somehow, Kyle was acting a bit too terrified, and he wasn't parting with whatever was in his hand.

"Naw, naw Ms. Preuss." He gripped it tighter.

"Sandy, what does he have?" Even Sandy couldn't speak. This concerned me further, but I purposely chose to keep Sandy out of it. She was a good kid. She was pregnant, and coming to school every day. She had given me 110% on her studies and behavior since she had come into my class. However she was involved, her demeanor, and Kyle's, demonstrated that she was not the guilty party.

"Ok, Kyle, outside," I said.

"Naw, Ms. Preuss, Naw, please." I'd never seen him like this. It was too small to be a pornographic picture or embarrassing note; I really thought it had to be something to eat. Why was he making such a big deal?

"Ok then, just give it to me, and it'll be over."

"Naw, please, I can't."

I was tempted to get Sandy to tell me, but again, something told me to leave her out of it. I didn't want her to be involved unless she really had to be. I just pretended that I hadn't even noticed that the item, whatever it was, had come from her hand into his. Kyle wasn't one to take the blame for anything he wasn't actually guilty for, and he was sure acting guilty, so I kept focused on him. Never took my eyes off the boy.

I wanted to know what the heck he had in his hand that was making him sweat. Funny thing is, if he wouldn't have been acting so odd, if he would have put it in his pocket and said,

"I won't chew it now, Ms. Preuss, I'll save it for lunch," I would have bought it. He would have pulled the wool right over my eyes, but he was so in the hot-seat, I knew there was more to this that met the eye.

"Outside," I said. He still didn't move.

"Get your butt up now, and walk it out that door, Kyle."

I couldn't believe my eyes, he still didn't move.

"Listen to me. You get your bony behind up and out that door right this minute." (I had learned from previously working two years in inner city schools that sometimes the use of such verbal visuals was helpful to actually get the response you were requesting.) I pointed to the door, and stared him down. Finally, he moved.

Once outside things only got worse.

"Give it to me, Kyle," I said, hand stretched out in front of me.

"I can't."

"You can and you will."

He was doing the oddest thing. He was on the verge of tears, but laughing at the same time. I'd never seen anything like this. This was just weird. I knew it had to be something very embarrassing. Things raced through my mind. A condom? A used condom? A folded up picture of some strange pornography? A tiny scull? A little pentagram? *Something along those lines.*

"End this now and give it to me, because I'm going to get it one way or another." He held it behind his back.

Kyle was a tall boy, tall as me. 5'10 or so. Thin as a rail. I was ready to wrestle him to the ground if I had to. That's how badly I wanted to know what was in his hand.

"Kyle, I'm going to reason with you. So listen to me now." I went on slowly. "Whatever it is, if you give it up now, things will go better for you. So take a second to think this through. You know me. I'm straight. I won't lie to you. I can't let this stand the way things are going down right now. I'll call whoever I need to down here to get this out of your hand, or maybe I'll knock you to the ground myself right here by the window so everybody can see." I could see the sudden fear in his eyes as he deliberated whether or not I'd really do that.

"Or you can hand it over. I promise you, handing it over will cause you the least amount of grief, and will give you the most support from me when we decide what it is we're going to do about it." I was trying to speak in as threatening a voice as I could possibly muster. There was that whole teacher-like psychological warfare effect going on in my voice as I tried penetrating him through the honest-to-God steel in my eyes.

He took a deep breath. He knew I meant it. I'd be there for him if he gave it to me willingly.

"Okay," he said, "But promise me you won't tell on me."

"I don't know what you've got, so I can't promise you that. I can only promise you that ticking me off any further will only complicate matters. If you hand it over, you're road will be less rocky."

By now, even I knew it had to be something other than a condom or a pornographic picture. But what? Something stolen from me? From another student? What was in his hand??

While Kyle and I continued with our logical pursuits trying to reason with each other, the entire class could see from inside the classroom. There were big windows and we were just outside. I saw the outlines of all my other beloved ones, watching intently as they remained, oddly, seated and quiet in the room. I knew that however I handled this would be remembered and would set the tone for the rest of the year. I tried to hold it together, but there were times when things got comical. Kyle is a funny guy. Actually, it was hard to keep straight about this, but I tried.

Just when he agreed to hand it to me, he had a second thought, and tried to make a run for the large garbage can down the hall. I put my whole body in front of him, grabbed him, grabbed his hand, and started prying it open. I think at this point I might have actually started to laugh. He was so shocked, he started to laugh again. And cry again.

Fortunately Kyle and I had begun to build a mutual respect for each other. When he realized I wasn't going to let him squirm out of this, he said, "Okay, Okay, Ms. Preuss," and opened up his hand.

I was shocked when I saw what he had. It was marijuana. It was the tiniest little bag of weed I'd ever seen. Back in the eighties, something this small was unheard of. I don't think I've seen a bag of weed since then. I didn't know there were even zip lock bags this small.

I looked at it and my heart fell. I was both shocked and disappointed. I never imagined drugs being passed in my room, in plain sight, in the course of instruction, as a possibility even for my students. That never entered my mind.

"This, Kyle? This is what you're passing in my class? I thought it was bubble gum or a condom or some other fool thing. How on earth could you be this stupid? Passing weed in my classroom? *Have you lost your mind?* If I could, I'd slap you silly right now. I mean if I thought I could whack you in the head a couple of times and not lose my job, well, that's just what I'd do."

"Go ahead Ms. Preuss. I deserve it. Do it now. Right here. In front of everybody."

"That would be too easy. Plus I like this job. Think I'll keep it, thank you."

"Just throw it away Ms. Preuss, no one has to know."

"Kyle, this is serious! You brought something illegal to school, and you violated my trust in you by passing it around in my room. Even if I wanted to, I can't pretend this didn't happen. People in that room, maybe the whole class, knows what went down by now."

"Yes, you can. Other teachers have done that. They just throw it out. Nobody knows." He was pleading desperately. I'd never seen Kyle like this. It was quite a sight.

"Kyle, I think you know me well enough to know *I'M NOT ONE OF THOSE TEACHERS*." I put my hand on his shoulder. He looked like he needed a hug. "I'm not going to call the cops in here, but at lunch time you and I are going to the office, and you're going to take care of this like a man."

"You'll stay with me, Ms. Preuss?" He grabbed my hand and held it in the oddest, neediest way. "Don't leave me alone." He was desperate. He looked in my eyes like he's never looked in my eyes before. "You'll stay with me?"

I softened. It was a moment that transcended anything I'd ever felt for a student. "Yes, if you want me to stay with you, I'll be right there. I promise."

Now it was time for lunch, and my whole class had been inside watching this 10-minute drama unfold outside the door. I had put the weed nonchalantly in my pocket as if it were a piece of candy. Then I walked back to the door, and just like any other day, I went back in the room and said.

"Okay, lunchtime! Everybody out, straight and quiet." They were all so stunned I didn't hear a word out of them. I was certain Sandy had told them what it was he was hiding, and they knew I had confiscated it, so there wasn't much to say.

One student finally broke the silence as we walked to lunch. "What are you going to do, Ms. Preuss?"

"Kyle and I will be taking care of the matter in the office. Don't you worry."

"Is Kyle going to get in trouble?"

"That would be a good guess."

"Is he going to go to jail?"

"Not if I can help it."

Kyle's eyes welled up. He was walking right next to me, stoic, no expression, slow in his step.

'You're going to stay with me, right Ms. Preuss?" He asked again.

"For as long as it takes, Kyle."

Inside the office we went straight to the administrator. Luckily Ms. Rodriguez, was sitting right at her desk. She knew by the look on our faces that something big was up.

"Can I close the door?" I said. She nodded. Kyle sat down. Kyle was never quiet. Kyle was always blabbing at the mouth with some comic or morbid agenda. It was so odd to see him sit there, quiet, not acting out, not defending himself, just sitting, waiting to see what I would say and do.

"Ms. Rodriguez, Kyle made a big mistake today. He was passing this in my class." I pulled the small bag of marijuana out of my pocket, placed it the center of her desk, and then I sat down next to Kyle. He still didn't speak, as she opened the bag, smelled it, and looked at us seriously, but he did something that surprised me. He pulled his chair close to mine, grabbed my hand, held it tight.

For thirty minutes he held my hand, wringing my fingers between his. When Ms. Rodriguez left us alone to go get Officer Duncan, the police officer assigned full time to our school, Kyle put his head on my knees, and he wept. Wept and babbled about how foolish he'd been and how I was not to leave him alone. It was perhaps one of the most important moments of my career. He *needed* me there and he wasn't afraid to show it. He calmly rested his head in my lap, as he squeezed my hand with his. I rubbed his back a little. It was the oddest, yet the most profound moment, almost as if he were my own son.

"Officer Duncan," I said as he walked in, "Kyle handed it over freely, and he told me how he got it. Can you please go as easy as possible on him?"

The interrogation lasted fifteen minutes and Kyle held my hand all the way through, often searching my eyes for support. It was grueling to watch as this self-proclaimed, "tough guy," showed his soft side and his fear, openly. I made a written statement about his helpfulness in the investigation and my recommendation that he not be arrested. He wasn't, thank God. He had already learned his lesson, and the amount of marijuana was very small. Between my favorable report and his mother's support in the matter, he was instead suspended for ten days and had to go to a drug rehabilitation center as part of his punishment.

He returned to my class a new man. This event affected him to the core. It had affected both of us. Kyle and I had a new relationship. One born of trust and respect.

From that day on, he was never a problem in my class. He never acted out again; he tried harder to do his work. I had seen a side of Kyle I never knew existed, a side I liked quite well. With all his bravado, and the scare tactics he loved to use on his teachers, he was a sweet kid with a heart of gold, and a mother who loved him and was there for him. That was his saving grace.

KYLE'S JOURNAL

Today for my journal I'll be writing about my lifelong lesson that I learned the day I was caught carrying weed in school. I learned many things from my experience. To tell you the truth it was scary as hell. Believe it or not, but you'll never want to get caught up in something like this. You'll also be known as a troublemaker for the rest of your life.

The many things that I learned from my experience is that once you get into trouble, most likely your so called friends won't be there to back you up. Another thing I learned is that it doesn't help your appearance upon others. You'll just be the biggest loser. If you think you're getting away with it now, just wait until later because it's going to come back and bite you in the a**. You'll feel like an even bigger a**hole because when you think that your friends got your back, it's just straight bullsh**. They are not there to help you, they just want you to make a stupid motherf***er of yourself.

It was scary as hell. When I say that, I mean I was pretty damn close to sh**ing in my pants. Especially when my so-called homeboys were not there to back me up. That was the most scary part of the whole situation. That'll take part in your situation if you want to go and be a stupid little a**hole as I chose to be.

So hopefully you'll be smarter than how I chose to be in a situation such as that one. Man, now I got a ton of people coming up to me every day, asking me if I regret what I did. I feel bad because it's not helping me look cool. Instead it's starting to help me look like one of the world's biggest f*** ups. So I trust that you'll make the right decisions in life.

In conclusion, I trust that you will not let somebody trick you into something that you don't want to do. Something that you know will get you in some sort of trouble. Something that would get your family members pissed. Don't always think that your friends are going to be there for every little thing that you go through. Your friends ain't always going to be around like your family. Always remember that.

KYLE'S AUTOBIOGRAPHY

My most painful moment in my life was when I found out that my father wasn't going to be coming home to me anymore. My father was murdered by five of his so-called homeboys.

Four days before my birthday, and five days before my dad's, when the news was brought to me. It was just another thing to add to my dark world. The news had a big impact on me, because I really loved my father for what he was. Even though he did what he did, nothing changed the fact that he was my father. I really hated the fact that he sold drugs. If you ask how I knew what drugs were at the age of six years old, you'll be surprised to know about what I knew at the age of six. I started to do good in school all the way up to second grade when I started telling people to f*** off. After he was murdered, I just really didn't care who I was saying that to. At around the age of 10 years old was when I started to think a lot about suicide, because that's how bad I wanted to be with my father. At the age of 14, I met the most wonderful teacher ever, and her name is Mrs. Preuss. I think that she is the greatest. Thanks to her I want to keep striving to stay alive. I thank her for that. But overall I really want to thank my family. But my new most painful thing is having Mrs. Preuss see what I go through in life. I really feel I should apologize for that. Thanks for taking your time to deal with me and my problems. Sorry if I've been adding onto the grief in your life that you just don't need.

I always ask myself, why did he have to die? Why isn't he here? Man, I need a dad. I need him to be by my side. Since he's gone nothin's right. Nothin's ever gonna be right. This concludes my journal.

* * *

Every day I read Kyle's words. Every day I grew to love him more. I began to understand him and see the genuineness of his spirit. He often went on and on about how I'd changed his life. Actually, I tend to think they weren't just words he knew I'd like to hear. I thought, even then, he really did mean it. I thought I did impact his life. And actually today, I know it as a fact. I impacted his life and he impacted mine. We have kept in touch all these years and are still very close.

He passed all his classes in high school that first year. I ran into his mother that year, she said, "He's doing great, Mrs. Preuss, it's like he's another person." We were both so proud.

But the following year Kyle began to do drugs again, get in trouble in school, and fight at school and after school. He wanted to be a, "tough guy," again, and started getting suspended for his unruly behavior. On his last day in high school he said a teacher "pissed him off" so he cursed her out good, then pulled the fire alarm and all the water faucets started up. He flooded the whole school that day. He seemed very proud of himself the day he came by to visit and tell me the story of how he'd been kicked out of his high school.

I was so sorry to hear about his turn for the worse. A year went by, and I got a call from Kyle, he had been in jail and met up with some of the kids he'd met in DOP. He read a few songs and poems to me over the phone and told me he was into some bad sh**, but that he'd never stopped writing since he left my class, and that writing brought him peace. He hung in dangerous circles a few years, but he would call me every six months or so, and I would put him on speaker phone and he would warn my DOP classes to take school seriously and not to end up like he had.

It became a ritual. He would call, and my classes felt inspired, and I know on some level he felt like he was helping the younger generation. He'd say the nicest things like, "You listen to Ms. Preuss if you know what's good for you. She knows the deal. I wish I would have remembered everything she told me. I wouldn't have ended up like this!"

I think he really made an impact on my future classes through those phone calls, and they never stopped coming. It was a curious continuation of the tie we'd developed when I was his teacher and he was one of my most difficult students.

One day he called from New York to tell me he'd gotten his GED, and was planning to go into the police academy. Today he is one of NYPD's finest. He is writing and producing his own music, which he sends me, so I can read the lyrics and hear the tunes. I'm very proud I know him.

Whenever he is in town he visits me at my school, in full uniform, and speaks to my middle school classes about his life and how he turned things around. The kids eat it up. They love when he visits. He and I have also shared the stage at the Florida League of Middle Schools Conference, where I presented to a conference of thousands of teachers on the strategies I use to succeed with troubled kids. He was there with a few other select students, and yes, he wore his uniform. He never neglects to mention the effect I had on his life, which makes me feel humbled, to realize I have made a difference in the world by making a difference in Kyle. That's the greatest reward a teacher can ever get. Ever!

I know I'll always keep in touch with Kyle. In some way, what we went through together spiritually fused us forever. It's one of those things that is difficult to explain, but just is. We grew to trust and respect one another both in class, and as people. That's rare, and beautiful, and it's the reason I do what I do. He taught me a lot about the meaning of being a teacher who could be trusted at all cost. It's a lesson I've taken into every classroom since, and I know students today appreciate what Kyle taught me about being a human being first, and a teacher second.

CHAPTER THREE

CHUNGO

One day early in that first year, I was teaching a lesson on personal narratives. I had the class read a personal narrative I had written about my mother and her life as an upper class girl in pre-Castro Cuba, and how it impacted my childhood. I told the class how proud I was that the *Miami Herald* published my personal narrative on Mother's Day, and how I surprised my mother by calling her and telling her that her Mother's Day gift was in *Tropic Magazine*, in the newspaper, that morning.

As I read the story, I started to cry. When I was finished, I told the class when that story was published, I felt like if I died the next day it would be okay because I had done something so wonderful for my mother. And, I'd had my "fifteen minutes of fame". Then I asked them to write a personal narrative of their own.

The class had one entire period in which to write it. They all seemed excited, and I heard many wonderful narratives read that day. When the bell was about to ring for break, Chungo was still writing. "Can I keep writing, Ms. Preuss, or do I have to go on break?"

"Of course you can keep writing. In fact, write until you're all done."

He wrote while the class was out socializing on their break, then he wrote for twenty minutes during our silent reading time, then he wrote for ten minutes during the announcements. After that he asked if he could read it to the class.

"Of course you can, Chungo," I said, and sat back in my chair, ready to listen.

His words held us all for almost fifteen minutes. There wasn't a dry eye among the girls when he was finished, including myself, and even the boys were speechless. I stood up and applauded. I couldn't believe what had come out of this child in the short time he worked on it. He blew me away. He blew us all away.

CHUNGO

I was born on August 1, 1985 in Providence, Rhode Island in a hospital called St. Joseph's Hospital. I was raised in Dartmouth Projects, a very rough place where they sold drugs, stole cars, and killed people if you messed one of them over.

After six years of living and passing through the stinky and unhealthy project halls, we moved to another place in Providence. My father and mother had saved up enough money to buy and build a house. We had moved into a three-apartment house where we had a backyard, a five-car garage and beautiful garden. It was so peaceful compared to the Projects. My father had bought me a dog cause now that we had our own house, we had more freedom.

As I got older, I met more people, did more things, had more fun and I was getting worse than just bad. In the fifth grade, I got suspended once for fighting. When I got to middle school, on my first year, I got suspended eight times. That's why I stayed back on my second year in sixth grade. I didn't get suspended, I just felt like not doing anything. I would mess around a lot, hit girls and did a lot of dumb stuff.

During half of the sixth grade, my parents broke up after they were married for 15 years. That really bothered me. Before I could even finish the sixth grade, my mother already had a boyfriend and we were moving to the Dominican Republic where he had a house ready for us. He was good for a while. Him and my mom got married. I went to school over there, where they put me to the seventh grade. I was going to stay back again, but they said I was too old for sixth grade so I went to the seventh.

I was not doing so good over there. I would fall asleep or I wouldn't listen or I would just talk all day, even during tests. Anyways, my mom and her husband broke up and we went back to Providence. We were living better. I was happier. When we got there, it was June 23, 1999. I used to hang out with my uncle ever since we were little. He used to come to my house to pick me up and we would go out chillin'.

One day, he had went to pick me up to go help him pick out some rims for his car, but that day I said naa. I told him I was going to stay home, that maybe I would call him at night. But something terrible happened. My uncle was shot four times in the head and twice in the chest. It was

July 18, 1999 at 5:45 in the afternoon when my mom got the news. When I found out, I got so depressed I would cry all day. I didn't even start school at the end of summer.

After all the drama, all I did was think about my uncle. That's when I got bad. It was like the devil was taking over my life. I would smoke weed every day. I would steal cars, I would hurt anyone even if they looked at me wrong. I even had a little ring to put dogs to fight for money. I was living a hard-knock life. I sold drugs and used to come home late and used to skip school. That's why I stayed back in the seventh grade again.

Then one day I was at the corner of my grandmother's house and I heard four gun shots. I ran towards the other corner, and I found my uncle's girlfriend laying on the ground in front of her house. Her little brother was laying next to her. There was blood all over. I got right next to them on the ground and I cried, but when I heard the sirens of the ambulance I ran home and locked myself up in my room. I didn't know what to do with my pants that were full of their blood. I was so scared, I stayed there in my room for a whole week, just thinking that it could have been me, cuz so many times I walked with them on that street.

I turned on the TV and I was watching the news and I had found out that somebody had killed her because she was witness to my uncle's homicide. All day the phone would ring. It was all of my friends finding out what had happened to me, and why wasn't I going out anymore. My mom always picked up the phone and tried to give it to me, but I didn't want to talk.

I know it was very bad in Providence. Every week someone would get killed. I would stay home and didn't come out for like a whole week. I only went to school and my other uncle would go pick me up in nice cars. He would make me feel safe every time I would walk in the street by sending one of the thugs that was in his gang to walk with me.

One day I was at home and my uncle from my father's side called my house, telling me and my mom to pack up, that we were moving to Florida. So I did just that. It was a three-day trip and we finally made it. When we were done unpacking the things into our new apartment, I did lots of thinking. I didn't want to die, and I didn't want to keep failing school. Anyways, I told my mom what I was thinking about doing with my life, and she brought me to this school, Destiny Middle, where I'm attending two grades in one. I feel good about myself because everyone is showing their love, I'm not falling asleep in class (only twice) and it was because my head hurt. I'm not skippin' school, I don't smoke, I don't steal, I don't sell, I don't put dogs to fight, I don't just punch no one anymore for no reason, and I don't come home late. I'm doing my homework every day except once, because there are times when I just think too much about my family back in Providence and my uncle.

Today I'm 15 years old, and all I have is positive ideas and a mom who loves me and a teacher who is like a mom, and the best teacher I ever had in my life. So when I grow up, I want to be a basketball player and that way I can make my uncle's tombstone the biggest one in Providence, Rhode Island. Today I have some crazy friends but they always show me love. That's why I'm showing it back.

With this letter, I want to tell everyone who's going the wrong way, just turn around and go the right way. And always talk to someone 'cause I never did until before I got here and you'll feel better after you're done telling them.

* * *

Chungo lived and thought like an honorable man, even when he was a kid. I always looked up to him for who he was and what he represented to the class. He was always an example and many of the kids from that year tell me how he changed their life. He changed mine too. He made me understand how much you can transform your life when you really want to.

He didn't make it through the traditional high school, but visited me often after graduating my class with flying colors. Then one day he brought me his high school diploma, laminated, which still hangs on my wall. He'd found a special school where he could do his high school classes faster than through the regular school system. He paid extra, but he said it was worth it.

I'm so happy I got to know him. I always respected him, and I'll never forget what he brought to my class, and the honor with which he always conducted himself in my presence.

His mother told me that even years after leaving Destiny, he still had hung all the awards and honors he'd received while in my class, in his room. That makes me realize I made a difference in a very special young man, who also made a difference in me.

CHAPTER FOUR

ASHLEY

I loved Ashley from the start. But, she could be explosive, volatile. She had a temper. Most of the kids feared or respected her. Nobody messed with her. Boy, could that little lady fight! She had gone after a few kids with her fists, and it always became a bloody event, usually causing permanent scars due to the fact that she wore a ring on every one of her fingers. Once, she tore so fiercely into a young girl after school that a rescue vehicle had to be called to take the other girl to the hospital. The injuries had been that formidable.

Everyone knew she would actually make good on her threats, and they usually backed off immediately rather than get into an argument with her. Once a boy in class said something she didn't like about her boyfriend, and she turned around and started beating the top of his head with a schoolbook. Her eyes went wild and she didn't stop until

I got there and held her back. The boy was just sitting in his seat protecting his head. I often wondered what could make a young girl act in such ways.

A few months into the school year, a distressing event occurred in her life. The one event that would change my life forever. The event that opened my eyes to so many things about the kids I teach. I'll let Ashley tell you about it.

ASHLEY

Hi, my name is Ashley and I'm fourteen years old and I'm going to tell you about the most terrible day I ever had. It started out great, and I had a good day in school and I handed in a lot of the make up work from when I was absent, and Mrs. Preuss checked my grades and she said I was passing and even had mostly A's. I was happy as heck about that cuz I never had no A's before, and I knew my mom was gonna be real proud.

Then in my elective class at the end of the day, I got called to the office. I walked in and I was still all happy about the news about my good grades, and they called me to this little room, and told me to wait there. I thought maybe my mom was going to pick me up early or something. Then this cop came in, and he was reading from some papers, and asked me was my name Ashley Banks and I said yes. And he waved his hand, that's how he tricked me, and that b**ch Rhonda, my social worker, came in. I hate her.

She had some more papers in her hand and she kept saying she had to take me to some courthouse right now. I was like, "I want to see my mother," but she wouldn't let me and the cop was trying to force me to go. I don't know this cop from jack, but I know Rhonda and I hate her. She's always poking her nose where it don't belong.

Well, I kept yelling that I want to see my mom, but they wouldn't call her and that damn cop tried to put his hands on me, and I pushed him away, so they called the officer from the school to calm me down cause I know him, at least, but I wasn't going to calm down for him either. No way.

I wanted to see my mom. You can't just take me someplace if my mom don't know where I am. I don't trust any of you and I'm not going no place without seeing my mom. If she says it's okay that I go, then I'll go. Not before.

I was making a fuss, and I got loud and everybody was starting to crowd at the door to see what was going on. All the administrators were there and Ms. Rodriguez, my own principal, came in and tried to talk to me. I was yelling at Rhonda, that phony b**ch, always trying to play like she cares about me, but she don't, she's a liar and she makes stuff up, and I couldn't even hear what Ms. Rodriguez was trying to say.

And that cop I don't know was acting all tough like just cuz he got a gun he can push people around.

I was like, get out of my face, Cop. I'm not going with you, and you don't scare me. Kill me if you want to. I'm not going anyplace with that lying two faced b**ch! I want to see my mom. Don't tell me sh** like you care about me. And don't flash no more damn papers in my face. I don't care what no papers say. "Kill me," I said. I'm not going with you!

Ms. Rodriguez asked me if she should get Mrs. Preuss and if that would calm me down.

And I was like, heck, yeah, at least she's straight and don't lie in your face. I kept thinking, hurry in here... where are you, Ms. Preuss? They want to take me away. I need somebody to help me. Don't let that b**ch take me.

Finally, Mrs. Preuss came and I was just holding her and crying and telling her everything what happened. And that cop was showing her the papers and said Mrs. Preuss would have to make me go with Rhonda. I had told her I wasn't going no place with Rhonda or that cop. She knows me. She knows when I say something I mean it. I wasn't going to leave unless they put a bullet through me, and took me in a bag.

I told Ms. Preuss, "Don't let them take me, I beg you! Why can't I see my mom? I just want to see my mom!"

Mrs. Preuss asked them why they couldn't just wait for my mom to come. She told them my mom wasn't far away. The cop and Rhonda kept telling her they couldn't wait and that it had to be done now, that they had to take me right then. I started to get hysterical and yell at Rhonda about what a lying two faced b**ch she is, and I told the cop again to shoot me dead if he wanted, that I wasn't going no place with him, and I was holding Mrs. Preuss and she was holding me.

So Mrs. Preuss asked the cop could he please ask Rhonda to step outside because she was making me so upset, and the coolest thing happened. The cop sent her out and shut the door in her face. Then the nice cop was there with me and Ms. Preuss and he was showing her the papers and she was asking him why this all had to go down like this since my mom was on her way, but he said there was nothing he could do, that when the courts sent those papers he just has to do what they say.

Then he gave her the papers and she sat next to me and was reading them, and she was asking me if I knew what it was all about. I told her my dad wanted me back and he was trying to get me away from my mom and I didn't want to go cause he used to hit me. I told her my mom was taking good care of me and I didn't want to go away from her and that I was happy here at school and that I never done so good in school, and I didn't want to leave.

So Ms. Preuss went outside with Rhonda and was asking her questions, and I could hear Rhonda telling her lies, so I started yelling to Ms. Preuss not to believe her, and Ms. Preuss came back in with me, and she sat next to me. She put her arm around me, and she said she was going wherever I was going, that I wouldn't be alone. She told me not to worry that if she couldn't stop them from taking me before my mom came, that she would follow me in her car, and be with me, and make sure I was safe.

All of that took some time and I was sitting there holding Ms. Preuss and she was still talking to the nice cop and Rhonda was trying to talk through the door, but she was still outside. Then finally my mom and my grandma came running in, since Ms. Preuss had called them on her cell phone cuz they wouldn't let me call. That was the happiest moment of my life when I saw them come.

My mom was talking to me and crying and she read the papers and the nice cop told her the same thing, that he couldn't stop it from happening. So my mom told me everything was going to be okay and that she'd take care of everything and that nobody was gonna take me from her. She was looking in my eyes, and holding me and she promised me that. So then I was ready to go.

Then the other cop came in, the one I didn't know, and he took me by the arm and he put handcuffs on me and on my feet, and I couldn't hardly walk. Then I had to go out like that and pass Rhonda, and Ms. Preuss, and all the administrators, and the kids, and all the people in the office. My grandmother started yelling at them all, and she got in the cops face.

"Why you gotta put them shackles on her. She's just a child!" She was yelling real loud in the office. She was crying real loud and they were rude to her and pushed her, and she was yelling at them some more, and they put handcuffs on her, and carried her away, kicking and screaming, so I couldn't see her no more.

Then they took me to the police car and put me in it all tied up like I was a hog or some other animal. They drove off, and told my mom she couldn't follow, but Rhonda followed.

I kept looking back to see my mom's car. But they stopped her from going. I finally realized I was all alone, and just kept wondering... *Why can Rhonda follow, but not my mom? My wrists hurt. My ankles hurt. Why are you tying me up? I'm not an animal. I didn't do anything wrong.*

Sometimes I would turn my head and I could see Rhonda, her ugly self, following in her car and I wanted to puke. I wanted to scream and I was already crying. I hate that lady.

I just wanted to be home with my mom and my grandmother. Tomorrow was gonna be my birthday. We are going to have a party at my house. I didn't want to be inside that stinking, greasy police car. *Where were they taking me?* I wanted to get out of the chains and cuffs. I kept praying... *Please let me go. Just let me go!*

They took me to this home for girls in Fort Lauderdale, and when I got there, Rhonda went to talk to some people at the desk and the cop and some fat, black, lady walked me up these steps without even getting me untied. I almost fell twice and they thought I was being difficult, and they kept pulling me back up, and telling me to, "move it!" and pushing me and sh** like that.

How the heck am I supposed to "move it" when my feet and arms are tied up in cuffs and chains?

I hated this place. At school they had told me, and my mom, and Ms. Preuss there was going to be a court hearing the next morning, which was my birthday, and my mom could pick me up then. Some birthday! They had lied, there wasn't no court hearing and I stayed there for three weeks and I never did get to see my mom, or have my birthday. So I have time to write in my journals so you can know what I been through.

They had us doing stupid sh** all the time, like go bowling and going to the hair salon where my hair got dyed really blond. And they had me in a room with this really fat girl who was nice, but she stank up the room cuz she peed her bed every night and they never would clean it up. I was always complaining, but they didn't give a sh**. So one day, I just told them I was getting the heck out of there and I just walked out of the front door and nobody tried to stop me.

I walked down the street and got on the bus and I went home. After a few more weeks, my mother went to the court and we took care of everything and now I'm living back with her for good. And my mom told the judge what Rhonda did and they told my mom the papers were wrong, and I didn't have to go no place with them when she came for me that day at school. So even the cops were full of sh** and my mom is going to have Rhonda fired.

* * *

In that instant I shared with Ashley, all the past 14 years I'd taught just vanished. Nothing else more clearly illustrated how much these troubled kids need a teacher's love. I knew then that what I was doing was special. It was bigger than teaching. I knew I'd found my niche. *These are the kinds of kids I can help. These are the kids I want to dedicate the rest of my career to. This is where I know I can make a difference.*

Ashley's event left me completely bewildered as I drove myself home that day without even knowing I was behind the wheel of a car. I was completely numb after the initial ordeal in the office, and watching her hobble off in handcuffs and shackles, connected by a thick chain behind her back, head down in shame. As I drove, I found myself reliving the moment her mother and I stood helpless at the curb and watched her look back at us through the dirty glass of the police car.

Her eyes had been fixed on us in a plaintive way, and filled with tears, and fear, and rage as the car drove away. They kept presenting themselves in my mind. I kept seeing those green eyes through the smudged glass window as she was driven to an unknown location, her arms held uncomfortably behind her. It is an image I'll never shake. Never. I felt I'd failed her. I had promised I would follow if her mom hadn't made it. But the police wouldn't let either of us follow. That night, I didn't sleep, just tossed and turned.

The next day several of the girls in the class brought presents and balloons for Ashley. It was her birthday. I had to keep from breaking down and crying right then and there, thinking about how she was locked up somewhere on her birthday, and knowing that her family couldn't even go to be with her.

I tried to hide my emotions and my concern.

"She's probably taking the day off for her birthday," I said into their smiling, excited faces. All the while my heart was breaking. I took the colorful balloons and gifts and put them in my storage closet. "I'll just put them in here for safe keeping. She'll probably be back tomorrow," I said, knowing I was lying. I didn't feel it was my place to tell them what had happened.

I tried to keep it together, but for days this affected me in my waking hours as I taught and related to my students, then at home as I tried to interact with my husband and children, then in my sleep. The image of her hobbling past in handcuffs and shackles, head down in shame, eyes filled with tears and terror, overwhelmed me. I got a little depressed over it, but I kept in touch with her family often. I had given them my cell phone number, and they knew they could call if I could help in any way. That was all I could do. But thoughts of Ashley permeated everything I did in such an intense way that it sometimes frightened me. I couldn't get her out of my mind, *How could this have happened to you? Where did they take you? Are you all right? Has this kind of thing ever happened to you before? I fear it has... I fear it's happened many times before.*

I understand now how I know nothing about your life. I understand how clueless educators are to the struggles our young people face today. And yet you come and sit in my class with your smile and your notebooks and you try so hard to be the student I expect you to be. You represent every child in school whose plight goes unnoticed and whose pleas fall on the deaf ears of inflexible educators who think they know something. We know nothing. Thank you Ashley for teaching me that we know nothing about the students we teach! And thank you for sending me on a journey to try to find it out so that I can teach with love and compassion and understanding. Things are so often not what they appear us, arrogant educators, who set our rules for you and expect that you can rise to the occasion. We think we know something and yet we know so little.

As the days passed, the kids at school were starting to ask what had happened to Ashley. I told them a rich uncle had taken her to Paris, and that she had sent me a post-card from there. The kids were skeptical.

"Really," I said, "I think I have one of the postcards on my desk. Pete, go check my desk." Pete went over.

"Nothing here," he said, moving papers around my desk.

"Well, I must have left it at home. I'll bring it tomorrow. She's having a ball, though, went to the Eiffel Tower..."

On and on I went, until they finally believed me, but my heart was panicked over what her real fate might have been.

I kept hoping she'd come back soon, but I really wasn't sure if I'd ever see her again. My heart felt the loss. I'd come to love her. She was one of those special kids I felt I could really touch, do something for, and impact in a lasting way. But she was ripped from my class and the support system she'd developed there, just as surely as she was ripped from the home and mother she knew and trusted.

Although her family assured me that if they got her back she would be allowed to return to my class, I wasn't certain I'd see her again. I feared her mother would lose the case, and that I would never see Ashley again. My thoughts raced daily... *How can they just steal you away? How can they think of returning you to a father who was physically abusing you? You don't have a voice in what they do with you. You don't have an advocate! You are a number in a system of faceless kids with case numbers and caseworkers who act like they care and don't really know how they muddle things.*

After a few weeks of being depressed and sad, I got a call at home one night.

"Ms. Preuss, it's me, Ashley."

I could hardly speak. "Where are you?" I stammered into the phone.

"I got out."

"What do you mean? Is everything okay now?"

"No, they're looking for me. I ran away."

"How could you do that, Ashley! Won't this hurt your mother's case?"

"I couldn't stay there no more, Ms. Preuss."

My heart sank. She told me all about the horrible experience and then how one day she just walked out of the front door and now she was in hiding.

"Be careful, Ashley. I don't want you getting yourself in any trouble."

"Don't worry about me, Ms. Preuss. I only called so you could tell me what work I can do to keep my grades up. When I get back, I don't want to be too far behind."

That was it. My heart leapt. It was one of those moments, that as an educator you never forget. I held tight to the receiver, knowing I'd gotten through to her. For once, school really meant something in her life. My work in DOP wasn't in vain. I had touched one life and I knew it. I couldn't believe that with all this little girl was going through in her life, she actually called to find out what work she could do for my class. But that was Ashley. From the moment she walked into my class, she did everything she could regarding her schoolwork to make me proud of her.

I actually did tell her what we were doing in class, and what chapters she could read if she could get to her books. I asked her not to tell me where she was because I didn't want to know if anyone ever asked me. When she walked back into my class, almost a month after the initial incident, she came with a notebook full of makeup work, which she proudly placed in my hand, her eyes stuck on mine, and a big smile on her face.

I'll never forget that first morning she came back. I had run into her in the parking lot. Her mom just happened to pull up in the car next to me as I walked into school.

"Ms. Preuss, Ms. Preuss!" I heard an excited voice yelling my way. I looked over to see Ashley in the back seat of her mom's car with a big smile on her face and looking as beautiful as ever. Her mom was beaming. "She's all mine, Ms. Preuss. I got her back!"

I was so happy to hear that! I knew that was where Ashley wanted to be. She bounced out of the car and into my arms. It was over. Whatever custody suit her father had attempted, or whatever that social worker Rhonda had done to try to take her away from her mother, they had lost. All that was for nothing, yet it will leave its scars on Ashley, and it will leave its scars on me... forever.

When Ashley came into my class after going through the office that morning, I called her aside and told her what I'd told the class. "They think you were in Paris. You don't have to tell them anything."

All the kids were curious, and in my class, we don't ignore the obvious, so eventually I gave her time to tell her story. *Story Telling Techniques* being a part of my Language Arts curriculum, she started with an imaginary adventure through the streets of Paris. At first she was laughing and having a good time making up events that occurred with her uncle in France. But in the end, she leveled with us all, and told us the harrowing experience in detail. The whole class sat on the floor, riveted, for almost an hour, as she sat on the rocking chair and went on and on about her terrifying experience and her time in the girl's detention center.

She was so animated as she proudly recalled the final details, "Then one day ... I just got fed up with those stupid, lying people. Especially Rhonda, I knew she lied to my mom to get me in there. So I said to them, 'I'm gonna walk out that door', and I did."

"Did anyone try to stop you?" one student asked.

"Nope," she said. "I just walked right out the front doors, and I just got on the first bus back home. Then I hid out with a friend until my court date came."

"Damn, girl! You been though some deep sh**!" Tony remarked, and went to hug her.

She was back. I was so glad to see her. That was early in the year, around November, I would guess. So many more things happened that would create a lasting bond between myself and Ashley, but those things, I'll keep locked in my heart forever.

We keep in touch to this day. She married a nice guy, lives in Kentucky and has two beautiful kids. She passed my class in spite of her explosive temper, which caused her to get in trouble with other teachers, and in spite of the occasional, yet memorable, fights that always landed her opponent in the hospital.

Unfortunately, she dropped out of high school before she even got her first report card. "I could make it there if you'd follow us to high school, Ms. Preuss," she would often say. If only she knew how I wished I could. A few months after dropping out, I spoke to her, and she was hoping to get home schooling from a friend of her mother's, but that didn't work out.

"You know me, Ms. Preuss. I can't take nobody getting in my face. Them teachers in high school are no good. They always want to get in your face. I'm gonna get home schooled, that way I got a chance to pass and finish high school."

She never quite made it, but after leaving Florida she got her GED and today is studying in Kentucky while taking care of her husband and raising her kids. I'm happy to know she has moved on to a better life.

CHAPTER FIVE

RAFE

RAFE'S JOURNAL, 7:45 AM, NOVEMBER 2000:

Well, I'm mad because I'm leaving this school today. I'm not ready to go. I love this class. I met so many new people here. I have some real close friends at this place, and this class is real tight. But they don't want me at this school here cuz all the parties I throw at my house and all the crazy stuff they think happens there.

So they made me a deal and I'm leaving and they moving me to the next grade. At my new school I'll be in 8th grade even though right now I'm still in seventh. That's a good deal cuz I failed three times, once in elementary and twice in middle school, so this will help me on my future and get me closer to my own grade with people my own age. Everybody tells me I'm too big and hairy to be in the seventh grade. Maybe they right, and tomorrow I'll be officially in 8th even though I'm supposed to be in 10th.

So my class be throwing me a party today. Everybody brought food. I see cookies and soda and chips on the big wavy table in the back, and Ms. Preuss bought a cake that says, "Good Luck, Rafe!" with a smiley face on it. I really don't want to be writing now. I just want to go and grub and have some fun all day, but we have to wait till we do all our work and we get back from lunch, then we can eat and have a party. We are going to play music and everything, and I borrowed a video camera my grandma got for Christmas from my uncle. She told me I better be careful with it. She care more about that camera than she care about me.

She never trust me with nothin', so when she said I could bring it, I was so happy. I promised her I would take good care of it and she was rewarding me, I guess, because I done so good in the DOP class and my good grades were getting me up to the eighth grade. She said, "I better get it back in one shiney a** piece," just like it looked when she gave it to me. And she told me not to let anybody touch it, so I don't care who asks me if they can use it, my answer will be no. Even if a hot a** girl asks. The answer is gonna still be no, even if she promises me some fun in the hot a** sun.

Maybe Ms. Preuss can use it a little bit so I can come out in the film. LOL! But only her!

I'm tired of writing already, Ms. Preuss, but I know I have to write another eleven minutes, and today is one day I don't want to upset you, not even a little bit, because I want things to go smooth till my party.

I can't wait till we get back from lunch. It's going to be so much fun. It's going to be a good day in school, then after too, 'cause a bunch of us from class are meeting and we're gonna hang out all night at my house while my grandmother is working. She never knows because I know how to clean up good after my parties. I'm tidy like that, and I makes my homies clean up too. I make them show my crib the respect it deserves. Know what I mean? So, yeah, it's going to be a great last day at this school for me today. We gonna party all day and then all night too.

Ms. Preuss, don't get mad at me when you read this, but I'ma tell you this because I know you won't read this till I'm gone. Ok, so here is a secret you don't know. See how my camera is on my lap. I been filming everybody writing this whole time. I got J.J. picking his nose, and Dalia's pink undies, and Rivo shot me a middle finger, and Kiko is making funny faces in the camera when you ain't looking, and I even got you grading some papers and drinking your green spinach juice. Maybe I'll tell you later and we can watch it and have a laugh, but I know, I think you'll make me erase it, so not till after the party.

Definitely not before, just in case you you wanna go, "Middle Aged Cuban Woman" on my a**! I don't want that today. Your eyes look like they coming out your head when you do that, and your neck gets all red and them veins come out. And you know, I can say it today since it's my last day. You get to saying some mad fierce wicked things that make my head wanna hide up into my neck like my turtle do when he's scared! You are a funny teacher, but a scary one too! At least I respect you. I never respected nobody else like I respect you.

Maybe I can tell you all this after the party. If not, I know you be reading this when I'm gone. Thanks for all you done for me. No one else gave me so many chances, and no one else ever let me be me, and not judge me, and yell at me for nothing all the time. You're the only one made me feel like I could make something of myself. One day I'll make you proud. You'll see. I promise. And I'll keep in touch 4eva!

RAFE'S JOURNAL, 9 PM, WRITTEN AT THE JUVENILE DETENTION CENTER:

Hi, my name is Rafe. Today I did some stupid sh**. I had brought a camera to school because it was gonna be my last day. My teacher had a party ready for me. Everybody brought chips and Coke and cookies and stuff, and we were gonna party after lunch and hang out and I was gonna film everybody to remember them all. Ms. Preuss told me I couldn't take the camera around, but I took it to lunch because she kept telling me I had to keep everything "G" rated, so I wanted to take it outside and have a little fun. So then I hid it in my bookbag and took it to the cafeteria, and got some good times at lunch on the video and we was going back to class when Takesha got into a fight with this girl, Tameeka. Sister just came up behind her and punched her on the head and pulled out her weave. Takesha wasn't having that, they had beef from way back, and Takesha jumped her and got her real good on the nose and forehead, so I wanted to film her. It was a damn good fight.

Everybody told me to put the camera away, all my friends did, but I thought I could get away with it, so I just held the camera up in the air and I filmed Takesha fighting Tameeka. It was funny. Now I see how stupid I was. I was a plain fool. People saw me doing it. Even Mr. Redmonde, one of the assistant principals at my school, came after me.

I hid it, bent down in the crowd, and tried to get back to my classroom, but he knew where I was. Us DOP kids stick out because we bigger and meaner looking than the rest of the kids at this school, so he busts right into our class a minute later, his big ugly self in there while I'm talking to Mrs. Preuss, and he starts acting like he's some wise a**, all tough and sh**, asking for my camera right in front of everybody.

But I didn't want to give it to him. My grandmother had lended it to me and there was no way I was giving it to that man. He was getting in my face and he wouldn't take no for an answer. He kept at me. Poor Ms. Preuss didn't know nothing about the fight yet, I was just getting started telling her. And he comes in with his big mouth, and all them whiskers he calls a beard, yelling and yelling and grabbing for the camera till he backed me back in my corner where I sit and I keep my stuff.

It's just a little corner where Ms. Preuss puts me so I don't talk so much to everybody because I talk a lot and disrupt the class and I make everybody laugh and sometimes Ms. Preuss laughs too, but sometimes she gets mad, and I like it back there in my corner because it's private, but I can still see the board, so it's all good. I ran back there to put the camera in my bookbag so Mr. Redmonde wouldn't get his greasy hands on it, but he went back there after me, and he got me so I'm trapped in my corner behind a bookshelf, and he's yelling for my camera and I'm getting pissed and yelling back and he won't let me the f*** outta there. And he's pulling out his little walkie talkie and calling for back up and sh**.

So I'm heated and my mind is racing... Who the f*** does he think he is? He can't just take my stuff because he want to, can he? That's not right. F*** no. Get outta my face man. Get out my face. It's my grandmother's camera, man. Get away from me, man. Why you trapping me in this corner? You know I got nowhere to go, why don't you lay off. I'm in a f***ing corner man, what more do you want? Stop yelling at me. Who you think you are to yell at me.

I just wanted to get the heck out of there. And the whole class is going wild and Ms. Preuss is yelling at them to be quiet so I can calm down, and then she tries to talk to Mr. Redmonde, but he don't even listen to her, because he's too busy talking to me and to his walkie talkie, but I knew that man wasn't getting his hands on my sh** or on my grandmother's only camera!

I must have been yelling stuff at him because I kept hearing Ms. Preuss tell me to sit down and chill out, but I couldn't shut up, he was making me so mad. I wanted to just hit that son of a b**ch in the face and I almost did, I balled up my fists and I banged into him with my chest, and I stared him down eye to eye.

I think Ms. Preuss got worried I would really slug that mother f***er, because she came right to us and put her hand on my shoulder to calm me down, but I needed out of that corner where all the yelling was coming from. That a**hole thinks he's so powerful or something and he thinks he can stop me, but I knew nobody was getting my camera, specially not him! Especially not like that, come in screaming at me like he somebody. He ain't nobody to me.

I heard Ms. Preuss tell me to settle back, "Don't do this Rafe," she kept saying. "Sit down Rafe, or you're gonna mess up real bad." I saw what looked like panic in her face, but I didn't care, I just got out of there anyway. Busted out really, because he had me trapped behind a bookshelf. I just moved the whole damn bookshelf, pushed it away. It surprised the f*** out of him, but Ms. Preuss saw it coming, and she got out of the way to let the bookshelf move. It was on wheels so it moved real easy, and I left out the front door. By then the whole damn school was there. Every single principal and security monitor, and counselor was there, waiting outside or running towards our class.

I'm thinking... Why the f*** they all there? Why were so many people out to get me? It's just a camera, and it don't belong to none of them. So I ran out the back door of the school to the yard out back, and Ms. Preuss ran after me and she said, "Don't throw it all way Rafe. Today is your last day. You're going to be in the eighth grade tomorrow, don't throw it all away."

We were up by the fence and she managed to calm me down some. She was talking real sweet like she normally do, "Go back in there, play nice, don't say another word, and it'll be okay." I trust Ms. Preuss, so I came back in, with her, but then all them people were there. They was coming at me and Ms. Preuss, running in from every hallway, from all over the school, and I didn't know where to go and Mr. Spitzer, my counselor, started yelling in my face, his big, black self! I cursed him out good, and Ms. Preuss kept telling me to shut up. I guess I must have been yelling a lot of really f***ed up stuff back at Mr. Spitzer. I don't remember none of it right now. But I remember they was all around me yelling stuff, and I just wanted them to shut the f*** up and leave me alone on my last day there.

I tried to get away from Mr. Spitzer, and I saw Ms. Preuss crying and running after me. Then that cop came and he pushed me onto the window right in front of my class. He put my face up on the glass and all the kids saw me spread on the glass, and they saw when they put hand cuffs on me and took me away. I never felt so shamed in my life. It was gonna be my special, fun day. I could see all the chips and cookies and soda and stuff Ms. Preuss had got ready for my party through the window when my face was pressed on to it. I couldn't believe this sh** was going down like it was.

I was thinking ... Why the f*** you gotta handcuff me man. I ain't no criminal. I ain't done nothin. Why you gotta do this, man?

Those handcuffs bit into my arms, I had them on a long time. They took my film. That's all I really wanted was to have that film. Now they got it. And I got nothing. When my Grandmother showed up, that was the worst part of it. She ain't like some other grandmothers I know.

"I don't care what you do to him. Take him to jail and charge him good. I'm moving to Ohio. He can rot in jail. I'm not even going to pick him up. I'm tired of him." She took her camera and left me there in them handcuffs.

Why that lady hate me? All she do is turn her back. She talks sh** all the time. She says I'm violent, says she's scared of me, and sh** like that. She says I'm dangerous. She says that sh** to everybody. She stays at work a lot, so what does she know about me being dangerous? She don't stay home, but she's always calling the police on me. Every time she finds out I got friends over, she calls the police, and they raid our apartment and everybody has to go home. She never say she's happy I clean her house and keep it nice. I don't even do that much drugs, my friends do, but not me.

Kids need a place to hang together. And I don't much like being alone anyway, and she always be leaving me alone. I don't run the streets or nothing, my friends come to me. Everybody in this class been to my place. Everybody knows, Mi Casa es Tu Casa, I make them know they got a place to hang. That's all I ever done wrong. I ain't never done nothing to her. She sold me out right there. She took her camera all right, but she didn't give a damn about me. Said she wouldn't be picking me up. Said I could rot in jail. What the f*** kinda grandmother is that?

I wanted to cry, but I didn't want her to see me so I turned around. I guess I've done some stupid sh**. But she's crazy, and she makes stuff up, that's why the police and the school think I'm so bad. So tonight I'm in jail, and they let me write this. They're saying I have battery charges against me. I know I didn't batter nobody. Ms. Preuss kept telling us that anybody could press charges, even if we just brush up against them, or put one finger on somebody. Now I know it's true. Mr. Redmonde said I assaulted him when I tried to get out of the corner and when I leaned a little bit against him. But I never hit that man. Not once. This is one f***ed up kind of day. Started out right, but gone bad. How did that happen so easy? How things go from good to bad just like that?

I got nobody else, and my grandmother been telling me she gonna send me to child protective services since I was five when my momma left me. Maybe now she means it. Maybe now I finally gone too far.

* * *

Rafe was one of my funniest students. Everybody liked him. He kept us laughing all day long. No matter what topic I was teaching, he had a way to make funny comments that were actually on topic most of the time, and added to the lesson. I knew he was a comedian at heart, so I usually let him. I told him one day he could have his own TV show or be on Saturday Night Live. He was that funny, very talented socially, and in comedic awareness. I really liked having him around, and was proud of his achievements. He had bounced around from school to school until he found Destiny. I felt that I could see what others couldn't see behind his gruff exterior. I was proud that he was going on to the 8th grade. We had a lovely day planned for him. Then, just like that, I lost Rafe in the most abrupt and unpleasant way.

I was throwing him a party and he was so excited about filming his friends. He made a big mistake: he took out the prized camera his grandmother had lent him to film a fight. When they came for his camera, he couldn't hold it together. He was defiant, got verbally aggressive, and even physically imposing. Instead of backing down, saying, "I'm sorry" and handing over the camera, when administration came in to get it, he got defensive. I tried to shut him up, but he couldn't stop himself. It was sad to watch. I saw the unraveling of a young man I cared very much about. The saddest part was my inability to stop it.

Once administrators are involved, teachers are supposed to back off. That was the hardest part of it, me backing off, and watching a kid I loved ruin everything he worked so hard for over a camera. It showed me how, regardless of what we do for them, or they do for themselves, if there is an uncontrollable rage within them, nothing and no one can stop it once the switch in their head is flipped.

He wanted to defend his property and what he thought were his rights, and he went about it in the worst possible way. He looked like a cornered animal as he sought safety behind a bookshelf, in his corner. But instead, he became trapped in the corner that we had created as his private learning haven for months, and there was no easy way out.

I wanted to ask the assistant principal, Mr. Redmonde, to let me handle him. Mr. Redmonde meant well, but he didn't know Rafe, didn't know his prior record of getting kicked out of schools for beating kids up and defying authority, didn't know his strength or his rage. I knew, but I didn't know how to say it in that moment. I didn't know the right words to use and the situation escalated so quickly, was becoming so explosive, it was spiraling out of control. I was stunned. Such a nice party was planned, and now everything was crumbling before my eyes and in front of my entire class.

Rafe lost it, pushed up against Mr. Redmonde, and was not being the submissive student Mr. Redmonde would have liked. I think it's difficult for some educators and administrators to understand that a segment of the school population doesn't register them as the authority figures they see themselves as, and have traditionally been. So it was bound to happen, and finally, he made his move. He busted through us, pushed a bookshelf away, banged into Mr. Redmonde and bolted out the door. Too late for Rafe.

They had called in an emergency alert and every person with a walkie-talkie was there waiting. Rafe's eyes looked crazed, and I raced after him to stop any further complications, but when he saw all those people, he didn't know what else to do but try to make a run for it. He ran about 20 yards to escape out the back door of the school with his book-bag and his camera.

I ran out with him, he was up against the fence trying to climb it. I reasoned with him, "Look, you have to go back and face the music. You'll never get away. Let me walk you back in calmly and they might go easy on you." I managed to talk him back into reality for a moment.

He looked at me, and said, "Why did they do this to me?"

"I don't know, Rafe. I guess they wanted your camera, Sweetie, and you wouldn't give it to them. Once you start cursing at adults in school, it's over. You know that. Let's just go back in there and give them the camera." He looked at me for a moment and I saw his red, flushed face, and the perspiration under his eyes and on his nose.

"Come on. We'll do it together. We'll give them the camera, and it'll be over."

"Can we still have my party?"

My heart broke. That's all he ever really wanted out of this day, his party. I knew I could lie to him, but that's not how I operate, so I told him the truth the best way I could.

"Rafe, I'll be honest, I have no idea what will happen once we walk back in there, but I know this. They are giving me time alone with you to make you reason." He paused and thought for a moment. "If they wanted, they'd all be out here right now, but they are giving me this chance. I can only imagine that means they'll go easy if I bring you back peacefully. Just try to keep it together, and whatever you do... don't open your mouth. Don't say one word."

He thought that over for a while, and hung his head down. "Okay, you're right. I lost it in there. Here," he said handing me the book-bag with the camera. "Give it to them. I don't want no trouble on my last day."

"I'm proud of you. I'll help you however I can, but you are going to have to hold it together, Sweetie." I looked him right in the eyes. "Are you ready to go in there?"

"I'm ready."

"Not one word?"

"Not one word. I promise," he said, staring right into my eyes, wanting to believe it.

I took the book-bag from him, and walked him through the back doors with my hand on the center of his back. His head was down, he was perfectly calm at that moment. I thought surely, things would be smooth now. I thought perhaps he'd be walked to the office, and reprimanded and given his final walking papers out of Destiny. I hoped against hope they wouldn't take away his transition deal, but it was too late. Too much had happened and too many people in command were unaware of all the facts.

When we walked through those doors, all the people on the other side looked to me like the enemy. I wish I could have walked Rafe to the office quietly and let him receive his punishment, reprimand, suspension, expulsion, whatever it would have been, in private, just he and I and Mr. Redmonde. But as soon as he saw the crowd of authority, he started giving Mr. Spitzer some lip, using loud profanity, and then everyone approached him, grabbed and took him from me. I remember feeling so powerless as an educator at that very moment.

It all became a surreal scene at that point. He went from passive boy, to enraged animal. When he was grabbed by three security guards at the same time, he acted like a wild tiger, and seemed to roar at them. I felt like the trainer who loved her wild and dangerous animal. I saw the beauty in his untamed soul. I knew how to talk him down to passivity, but it wasn't in my hands anymore. The others had come in. I wished they would all go away and let me settle him down, let me do my job like I always did, like I had just done. There's a certain dance I dance with a child like Rafe, then he willingly does what I ask. It just comes to me, and I know what needs to be said. I know what they need to hear. But now, he was taken over by force. I felt like I had let him down, thrown him to the wolves.

With all the love I'd given Rafe in the months I'd had him, knowing his volatile and violent side and his arrest record, I had managed to keep something like this from happening. I thought I still could have reined him in, could have talked him down, pacified him one more time, like I did outside, or the many times when he'd have an outburst during class. But it was all unfolding so quickly. Everything that was happening was out of my hands. My worst nightmare had come true. To see a kid—troubled, yes, but with intellectual potential--throw it all away because he couldn't hold it together, because he rebelled against authority, broke me.

I couldn't make him stop yelling and cursing.

"Get the f*** off me. F*** all you F***ers." He managed to spring loose for an instant, I saw the hope in his eyes, but it was just for an instant, they grabbed him again.

Within seconds, he was spread-eagled and in handcuffs. Officer Duncan, our school resource officer, had him pinned against the large windows outside my room. The three security guards assisted. The biggest humiliation of all...the whole class was watching.

I felt crushed. I wanted to protect these kids. I love them. I show them all the respect and kindness I possibly can within the framework of discipline, and order, and tough love. Then in one instant, I witnessed months of work and nurturing go down the drain.

In reality, most of my students are like wild animals, beautiful and kind in their own environment, but loose cannons. It doesn't take much to set them off. I wish I could say the right thing in those moments to get the control back, to be the one handling things, like when my doors are closed and it's just us. I always knew he could pop, but he'd never popped with me. He'd been a model student, except for his need to be my class comedian. He'd never once shown our class that violent side that had haunted him at his other schools.

But it's out of my hands when the administration, or the police, or child services, or HRS, or the courts are involved. There's nothing I can do but sit back in horror and watch one of my babies unravel. Dig themselves into a hole because they don't know what else to do, because they don't know how to deal with conflict. They don't think. They act out.

Earlier, before all of this mayhem, I had wanted to say, "Mr. Redmonde, please go out of my room. I can handle Rafe. He'll give me the camera. Just let me do this. Let me talk to him." But the words didn't know how to come out so they didn't sound like insubordination on my part, so I wouldn't lose my job. So, I kept my silence, and talked only to Rafe. I wish now I could have said it. I wish I could have known how to ask Mr. Redmonde to please get out of my room and let me get the camera to him without any altercation. Mr. Redmonde would have let me, had I only known how to say it.

I need to find the way to say it. I have to let them know, when things are escalating, that if they would leave it to me, it would de-escalate. It's hard to know how to say the right words, but I have to find a way. The kids feel safe around me and they know that I will protect them if I can. I feel like I let Rafe down, and I never want that to happen again to any other student. Maybe I can have something ready to say next time like: "May I request permission to handle this in my own way? Tell me what you want to see happen and I'll try to make it happen for you. But please, let me handle my kids, they trust me." Yes, that sounds respectful enough. Next time I would be ready. I hoped never to have to see anyone come into my room again, and spoil the safety net I'd built for my students. I can thank Rafe for teaching me how to stand up for my rights as their teacher.

It isn't easy to tell an administrator to get out of your business, but I have done it a time or two since, in a very politically correct way, so I could save one of my students from what Rafe had to experience.

"Let me get him... I've got this, don't worry yourself... I know how to handle her, just let me take care of it." So many things I learned to say to save my students from having to face anyone other than me when they messed up. For that I will always thank Rafe. His unraveling gave me the courage to follow my gut, rather than protocol, in the years to come in order to protect my students from themselves.

After they got the cuffs on him and dragged him away, I got someone to cover my class, and I went to see Rafe in the office. He was sitting in a chair with a security guard to his right. I sat on his left. He was still in cuffs. There was a tear in his eye that he'd been unable to wipe off because of the cuffs.

"Do you want me to wipe that tear?" I asked him. He nodded, so I wiped it for him. He smiled a little.

"I messed up, didn't I Ms. Preuss?"

"Yes you did, Sweetie."

"I'm not gonna go to 8th grade am I?"

"I don't know, but I don't think so, Rafe. You made a lot of people really angry today. Those were the people who were going to help you transition and skip a grade."

"Yeah. Guess I should have listened to you and kept my camera in the room."

"Guess so, Rafe. I don't know what you were thinking! How did you think you could get away with that?"

"I don't know," he said. "I guess I wasn't thinking."

"Yeah! That's what happens when we don't think."

It was an odd, sad, final conversation. I sensed we both felt it was the end of an era. The end of his run at doing well in school. The end of his hopes and dreams. He was going to jail. There was no doubt about it.

I told him his attorney could call me if he needed me to tell them what I saw, but I also had to tell him that Mr. Redmonde had the right to press charges. Rafe is almost 6 feet tall, and weighs at least 240 pounds. He's a mean-looking kid with a thick neck, muscled arms, a fuzz moustache, and big fists. Sure, he looked scary to some teachers, but he was the class clown and a big pussycat to me.

Battery charges were being filed against Rafe, on what would have been his last day in my class. The saddest part was that he failed seventh grade last year, so he was going to be transitioned to the eighth grade. That's one of the unique and special perks of being in my class. It's a transition program to do two years in one. I had just filed his withdrawal grades an hour prior to the incident. Three Bs, two Cs, one A. A letter had been drafted to his new school so that he could be transitioned into 8th grade. He was on his way to being an eighth grader. At 2:15 the transition would have gone into effect.

Rafe shot off like a cannon at 11:15.

No transition. No good report to the new school. A criminal record for battery. Time in jail. Turns out his grandmother never did pick him up.

* * *

THE CLASS' OPINIONS: Next day, round table discussion and morning journal excerpts.

TOPIC: Yesterday we lost Rafe, one of our favorite classmates and friends. How could his send off celebration have been more pleasant?

TONY

Mr. Redmonde could have just asked for the camera in a nice way instead of acting "all that" and demanding it in front of everybody. He could have explained to Rafe what was going to happen to the camera. If it was me I wouldn't have ever brought it to lunch, but it's a little late to do something about it now and dwelling on it won't help because he's in jail.

RAINEY

If I was Rafe I would have never video taped that fight. He should have listened to Rolando. He told Rafe to put the camera away, but he thought he could get away with it. Actually it was no biggie, I don't know why he had to get arrested. I mean all this was over a camera for heaven's sake. But he shouldn't have taped the fight in front of so many people. That's a sure way to get caught, and plain, bone headed stupid. And when Mr. Redmonde asked him for it, he should have just given it to him. Then he wouldn't have been so pissed and Rafe wouldn't have gotten arrested. I was so mad when the officer handcuffed him. That was unnecessary. Cops always want to act tough.

ROLANDO

If he would have listen to me none of this would of happen. I mean, I tried to tell him to put it away; he just didn't want to listen. He don't see it. I mean, I tried to help him, but some people don't take help. They just see things how they want. Now my friend's gone and they are charging him with some kind of lame charges like battery. I didn't see no battery. I just saw one angry nigga saying his peace, but he should have kept his fat mouth shut. That's what he shoulda done.

SA'RINA

I feel bad that Rafe had to leave, but he should have never rubbed up on Mr. Redmonde, and started cussin' him out. That's what got him in trouble, not the fight. If Takesha wouldn't have gotten in a fight none of this would of happened. There would of been nothing to film and we all could have had our party for Rafe. I was so sad cuz all the chips were ready and everybody wanted to say their goodbyes, and next thing you know all hell is breaking loose in the room and Rafe is cussing at Mr. Redmonde and then he runs out, and next thing I know, he's got on hand cuffs. And now he got a record for battery. Well, I don't want to talk about it anymore cuz I'll cry and it's too early in the morning for that. And all that food gone to waste cuz nobody felt like grubbing after what went down.

RIVO

He should have given the camera to the man and he won't get in trouble and go to jail. I saw when he took it out to film the fight and when a lady told him to give it to her and he ran away and she saw him put it in his bookbag, then they all came to our class. They told him to give up the camera, but he don't want to give it. And the man said if you give me the camera you won't get in no trouble, but Rafe won't give it and he said, "No, I'm not giving it up, you are not getting that camera cuz I said so and that's it." Then the man got the camera from Rafe's hand and he got so mad he tried to hit the man in the face. But then a police came and it was all over for Rafe.

CARLOS

I wish this didn't happen. It could have been us having fun and eating, and Rafe would have gone home happy and Takesha wouldn't have been in a fight and she wouldn't be suspended. But Takesha had to fight that girl and Rafe had to take the camera out of his bookbag because he's hard headed even when Rolando and Kiko told him not to take it out, he still did, and he held it up so high and everybody saw, and they was telling him to put it down, but he wouldn't listen, he kept it up high and kept on filming the whole damn time till he got caught, then he tried to run away, but it was too late. Everybody saw, and everybody knows Rafe's in the DOP class, so they know where to come and get him. If only Takesha could have just walked off, but no, she had to fight, and now all this has happened and Rafe's gonna stay in the 7th grade when he was going to go to the 8th.

TREVOR

I wish we could have had a nice party for Rafe like we planned. Instead of what we got which was seeing our Rafe get yelled at, seeing his camera taken, seeing him almost hit a principal, then last but not least, seeing him spread out on the glass in handcuffs and everything. Not cool. We all saw, and everybody likes Rafe. I don't know anybody that doesn't like Rafe. Everybody go to his house and have good times there, real good times. It would have been a great party yesterday. Instead, Ms. Preuss and all the girls were crying and everybody was sad and nobody wanted to eat and all the food got wasted for nothing. I hope he gets out of jail and comes back to see us, but I think that's the last we'll see of Rafe.

HAILEY

Rafe's send off celebration could have been so great if he never would have got arrested. Everything would've been fine if Rafe didn't take out the camera to film the fight with Takesha, but he wanted Takesha to fight so he could film it and he was making her want to fight the whole time and yelling stuff, and the fight was really funny. It looked like they were boxing each other in a ring, so I understand why Rafe wanted to get it on tape on his last day of school, because that was a cool memory of Takesha having a fight. He should have just kept the camera real low so no one could see it. Everybody was telling him to keep it down. Personally, he didn't even do anything wrong to get arrested. If anything, they could've at least not put handcuffs on him. I mean, he is no criminal. If it was me, I would have kept the camera down low and if an administrator still saw it, I would've given it straight to him when he asked, because the more you talk back and the more you refuse something, the more trouble you get into. But to tell the honest truth, most people in this class would have done the same stupid thing he did, filmed every little thing, yelled at Redmonde, etc., etc. But I wish he would've been smarter and not done any of that.

I'm really gonna miss Rafe. I feel really bad he's gonna have to stay in the 7th grade. I mean, if they promised him he'd go to the 8th grade when he moved away from the school, then why should one little thing like this have to change that? I hope he still gets to go to the 8th grade. And I guess it's not such a little thing.

* * *

Rafe wrote me some journals while he was in jail and sent them to us through a classmate. It touched me that he cared enough about me, our class, and himself, to do that. He had to be taken to a special home for juvenile delinquents when he got out because his grandmother wouldn't take him. A few weeks later, I heard he was moving to Seattle with one of his uncles to get away from the life in South Florida. I lost touch with him for a few years, but he called me the year he finished high school and was the defensive end on his football team. Later, I heard he played a year of college football, but he got into a brawl, over a bad call, with a referee. It got physical, charges were filed, and he got kicked off the team and out of that school in the first season.

Then something tragic happened and he lost his way. He moved to L.A. and started to sell drugs because he couldn't find a job with an assault record. A drug deal went sour one day and he shot a man. He's behind bars for a long time.

His uncle flew me out to Los Angeles so I could testify at his trial. I said every good thing I could think of saying about the boy I'd known, and how the cards were stacked against him. His high school football coach was there too. Apparently, he never once lost his temper, or got in trouble the whole time he lived in Seattle and went to school there. But it didn't matter what we said. He had a gun, he shot a man. It was over.

Just last year he wrote me a little note from jail. He thanked me for never judging him and for making a difference in his life. He said he was studying a lot in jail and he was going to get some sort of college degree there. He was hoping to get out for good behavior a little earlier than expected. I hope he makes it. That's what it's all about. You give love, you get love.

I have found through teaching that love never dies. It really doesn't. No matter how the lives of my students turn out, I love them still. I still see their smiles and bright eyes. And, I remember the good in them… always.

Rafe is not the only student who I loved that is now behind bars. There are many. Some for small crimes, and some even accused of murder. To my knowledge, at least four of my students have been convicted for manslaughter at the time of this writing. Many are in jail for drugs, gang activity and theft. One of my students is on death row and will never, ever, be let out of jail, another is in for 30 years. These are kids I'll always love, no matter what.

Love never dies, I've found that out.

How can I reconcile that I know and love convicted killers? Well, like I said, love never dies.

Everyone deserves to be loved. Even if they make horrible and tragic mistakes, my love for them never dies. It lives on in the way I remember them, in what I know they once hoped they could be.

Once love is there, it's just there. You can't turn it off or extinguish it because someone goes to jail, or commits a horrible crime.

I still manage to remember the best in them. I hold out, into my reality, the memory of who they wanted to become, and the hope they had when they were in my class, that they would have good lives and bright futures.

CHAPTER SIX

DIVORCE

Virtually every student in any of my DOP classes has been the child of divorce. That sends a powerful message. I'll say no more...

PETER

My name is Peter. A few years ago when I was eight, my parents were arguing a lot everyday, and mom was crying everyday, and they told me they were going to get divorced. I was very sad. My dad moved out and me and my little brother were living alone with Mom. Nothing was the same. Nothing was good anymore. They kept saying it was better for me because it wasn't good for me to live in a house with so much fighting. So for a year they were trying to get a divorce.

I kept begging them not to. I would talk to my dad about it when he took us on the weekend. Then I'd talk to my mother all week long. I told both of them that I didn't want them to get a divorce. I would cry and beg and get depressed. I would lock myself in my room. I even told my mother I wanted to kill myself. She got really scared. I don't know why anybody would think that I would rather have no father living with me than to have a father who is fighting with my mother. Of course I'd rather if they are together, however that is. I don't care if they fight. I just want my mom and my dad together.

So after a year they decided they wouldn't get a divorce and now they are together for some years and I'm thirteen and we all live together. I'm the only one in my class who lives with both his parents. I think that's very sad. Children need both parents, even if there is fighting. I think that's just a story anyway. I think they do it for themselves, not the kids. I think they just don't want to be together anymore, so they make up this thing about how it's not good for kids to have parents who argue. Well, it's not good for kids to have parents who are divorced either.

Every f***ed up kid I know has his parents divorced. And every kid I know who talks about it says their darkest time was when their parents split up. Mostly, my friends tell me they miss their dads, and they usually don't like their stepfathers. I only know one kid who really likes his stepfather and that was just because his dad was a real jerk and was in jail most of the time. Other than him, nobody I know likes their step dad, so I'm glad I live with my own dad now, because my mom is beautiful and I know she would have got married again, and I would have to live with some man I don't hardly know and just see my own dad every now and then, or maybe not at all. Like Juan, because his mom moved all the way to Florida and left his dad in New York. That's not right.

DAWN

When my parents got divorced everything changed for me. I lived in a house before and now I live in a crappy motel with prostitutes f***ing around in the rooms next door. I hate it. My whole life sucks. We used to have a car and now I take buses. My dad wasn't so great, I mean he wasn't my real dad, but he was my little brother's dad, and even though he didn't like me as much as he liked his own kid, at least he wasn't mean or anything. And now my mom and me are by ourselves cuz that was his house we were in, so my mom had to leave.

She went back to drinking. Maybe if she wouldn't have gone back to drinking we could still be in our house. I don't know for sure. She says she didn't start drinking again until we came to Florida, but I'm not sure she's telling the truth. I think my dad left her because she started drinking. He hates anybody who drinks cuz he used to drink and he stopped. So if you ask me, that's why they got the divorce. I think she was trying to hide it from him. At least that's what I heard people say.

DANIEL

My mom had to get divorced because my dad got caught selling drugs when I was a baby and she didn't want to live like that anymore. He's still in jail and I've never met him. He had other kids, not just me. But he only had me with my mom. My mom got married when I was five to a nice guy who is good to her. I don't blame her. My dad is a drug dealer, and when he gets out of jail he's gonna have lots of people after him because he snitched to get less time. My mom doesn't want me to see him. She says he's no good.

So I live with my mom and stepdad and my two little brothers, and it's okay. But I wish my own dad hadn't done what he done. I wish I could go and see him whenever I wanted like other kids, and that he wasn't in jail.

BOBBY

My step dad is a musician and he makes good money but he's out at night a lot. My mom gets jealous because he's good looking, but so is she. They go out sometimes to where he sings at and I have to stay alone at home, or I watch my little brother, he's only three. I don't like to be home with my brother because he's a little twerp and he doesn't listen to me, then he makes a big mess and I get yelled at when my parents get home, but it's not my fault. He doesn't listen to me. At least I put him in bed and get his diapers on and that. But I'm not gonna clean up all his sh**. So I let them get pissed.

RIVO

My mom got divorced when she was pregnant with me, which really sucks cuz I have no idea who my dad really is. Sometimes, I think she's lying to me. I think maybe she was never married to him and she just doesn't want me to know, but she says that's not true. She says he's just in Jamaica and he doesn't care about me. Like I want to hear that?

My mom is always having these a**hole boyfriends over and I can't stand it. We only have like a one bedroom apartment and I sleep in the living room, so I hear everything. Sometimes I want to go in there with a big knife and stab them till they stop making all the noise f***ing my mother.

She had a rich boyfriend when I was little. He was nice and I thought he was my daddy and he got her plastic surgery and her boobs are like gigantic so now every guy wants to go to bed with her. She's kind of a player. Even my grandmother tells me that. She and my grandmother don't get along.

I don't see why these guys can't go to their own house if they want to do it with my mom. Why do they have to come here? I mean they know I'm right there. Why can't they just go out some place. Maybe they think I won't know what they're doing cuz I'm just a kid, but I'm fourteen. It's not like I don't know what they're doing. Or maybe they are married or something, and my mom doesn't want their wife to find out. I don't know why. But I hate to hear that every night.

NIKOLAS

My parents are divorced. Aren't everyone's? My mom lives with the biggest jerk in the world. He's always drinking and he yells at us all the time. He says I'm stupid and I'll never amount to anything. I don't know why my mom stays with him. He's even hit her a few times, but she never wants to call the cops because she's scared of him. I think he's afraid to hit me because he thinks I'll hit him back. If I ever saw him when he hit my mom, I'd go at him for sure, but he does it when I'm not around. I'm not around much because I hate him, so I stay out as late as I can because whenever

I'm home, he's just yelling bullsh** at me and making me feel like I want to die. Sometimes I don't even go home. I stay with friends and party all night if I can, or crash at the beach, right on the sand.

My homies take care of me since they know my home life sucks. They give me whatever I want. But then in the morning I'm so f***ed up and tired I don't really want to go to school. But I'll get picked up and they'll take me to JIFF (Juvenile Detention) if I'm around the street, and the cops see me. So I just go to school and do the best I can there. But if some teacher gets in my face, things get nasty. I wish they would just leave me alone. At least I'm in DOP now and Ms. Preuss never yells at me for being late. I think the kids told her I sleep on the beach sometimes, under the bridge.

RAMON

I was a good student until the third grade. Well, I'll be honest, I never could spell or write good, but I could do math great and I was passing all my classes. Something terrible happened to my family in that year. My mom had an affair. She was out all the time and my dad didn't know for a long time. Then one day she was just gone. She took all her sh** out of her room, and out of the closet and left everything in a mess. Then my dad sat me and my brother down and he told us that mom had gone to live with some guy she fell in love with and it was gonna just be the three of us. That was the most f***ed up day of my life. I thought she would come back, but she hasn't yet and it's been four years. When she broke up with that guy, she just went with another one, but she didn't come back home. My dad kept saying he would take her back, but she wouldn't come. After that is when my grades went to sh**. I don't care about school. I don't care about anything.

ALEX

I was totally bummed over what happened this summer with my mom. I went to see her in Kansas City and she promised me that she was gonna take me around and to see stuff, but she didn't. I spent the whole time with my grandmother just watching TV. I live with my dad since my mom can't take care of me good and I haven't seen her in so long, I thought she'd want to see me, but she don't. She always had this and that to do. Then on the last night when I was leaving the next day, she promised me she was coming over and we would go out to dinner. I got all dressed up and I even put on some of my cousin's cologne and he lended me a tie so I would look older. I waited and waited and she came late and I was hungry by then, but my grandma had made me a sandwich so I could wait for her. She finally came and her and my grandma started arguing about how could she be late and sh** like that, but it's all good, at least she came.

Just when I thought we were gonna go out, she got a call from some of her friends that they were dancing somewhere and she just took off to go dancing with them. So I don't have no mother no more. She don't want me. She don't care, so I don't need her for nothing. She's dead to me.

TONY

If I could erase one event from my life I think it would be when my mom and dad got a divorce. When they told me we were going to have a divorce, I was sad because I had some friends whose parents were divorced and they told me it was a bad thing. So when they told me that I went to my room and locked the door and didn't come out till the next day for school. When I got to school, I went up to my friend Jonathan and told him about what happened and he answered back with, "welcome to the club." I was sad, but 5 years later my mom and dad got back together and we were together for about one year and then he died of a drug overdose from something my uncle, my mom's brother, gave him. That sh** is messed up, but what can I do about it? Now I really got no dad.

TONY - WRITTEN IN 2000 AS AN ESSAY ASSIGNMENT ABOUT DRUGS

I was asked to write an essay about drugs for my teacher. Now, in the back of my head I was saying, ``Yeah right." But I wrote one anyway because I know the real deal about what goes on with drugs, like destroying your brain, and the simple fact they consume your life entirely.

You're probably thinking, "This kid has no clue what he's talking about." Well, just for the record, I know just as much as you, and maybe even more. The only reason for that is because drugs took over a part of my life.

The fact is that if you do drugs, you won't stand a chance at life, or anything good that comes along with it. If you're wondering how that happens, it's fairly simple. The drugs you're using (whatever that may be) will start to eat away at your brain. Most of the time the "high" is just your brain telling your body it can't breathe. That type of "high" is almost the same feeling as your brain drowning in drugs.

When I said drugs took over a part of my life, I meant it. I remember when my father and I would go out for the night or play catch for a while. That type of stuff doesn't happen anymore. My father was a heroin addict. One night we got into a huge fight because he called my mother the "C" word. I yelled at him, "I hate your guts and I want you dead!" That's when I got sent to my room. I could hear my parents talking in the other room, and mostly they were talking and yelling at each other about me.

The next day my father went to work and he never came home. My father had died of an overdose of heroin. That fight was the last time we spoke.

This really had an effect on my mother. To this day, she cries over everything that happened on the 22nd day of March, 1997. And, nothing in our life was ever the same.

The only reason I told you that story was to tell you how drugs consume your life, and then take it from you, without you even knowing. If you're lucky enough or strong enough to quit using whatever you're using, then you should be extremely proud of yourself. And to those who are considering taking drugs, please don't make that mistake. Go to the library, find someone who knows, learn about it first!

You don't want to end up like me, listening to your mother saying, "Tony, I miss your father."

* * *

CHAPTER SEVEN

MORE VOICES

CHUNGO

His uncle's murder invades his thoughts daily.

Dear Uncle Emilio,

It's been one year and a month since you've been gone. Every day I sit back and reminisce on all the stupid stuff we've ever done. I miss you, everything has changed since you left. I wish I can change back the hands of time when we used to go and shop for clothes at the mall. Remember how we used to bet on dogfights in the basement?

Since you been shot, it's been nothin' but a hard knock life for me, you were the greatest. When you left I did nothin' but smoke all the week. I could hardly go to school and if I did I would just fall asleep or get into a fight for no reason.

I miss your lady too, so hopefully she's up there with you cuz it was terrible the way she died and she was only eighteen.

I cried every day when you left and still, till this day I cry and think of you as my first role model. I know you were into bad things, but God will forgive you for your sins. However, you know I'm gonna keep it real with everyone, like you did, on the streets of Rhode Island. Well as you can see I'm in Florida right now and I'm keeping it real down here with all these farmers, but anyways, you know I love you and I'll always keep you in my heart and if anyone talks shi** about you, I'm gonna set it off on them. However you would have, if I was the one that was dead. Anyways, I miss you and I'll see you when I get there.

Love, Chungo

P.S. Please write back from heaven if you can.

RAINEY

This young lady's mom was left paralyzed after a car accident.

Dear World:

My name is Rainey and I'm going to tell you a little about what goes on in a child's mind. First, we hate it when you adults try to make our choices (it makes us feel like a baby). And usually we know better than to do things that are wrong like take drugs or have sex. But sometimes we just want to be kids and not have adult responsibilities.

Like taking care of a mother who can't walk. And not having a father figure in your life. Like living on the streets cause your mom can't work. And stealing food because you are hungry.

We are saying that if you would take care of us and try to be better parents that we'll have time to be kids and not, all the time, have to be adults and do adult things like help you around the house to cook and clean and take care of the yard. Because we just want to be a kid.

This journal is a cry for help from an eighth grade DOP student. Because you forgot that you already had your life, but mine is just starting, and it's not fair that I don't ever get to be a kid. I want to be a kid. That's all.

LATOYA

She shares more about her painful experience.

Sometimes I just feel like dying and getting away from this problem of mine. I thought that if my mom didn't care when her boyfriend was molesting me then why should I care. I wanted so many times to just kill myself, but I never did it. (Only because it's a sin!)

But being molested was the most painful experience in my life. After that I always wanted to play by myself and be alone and I hated everyone around me because the person who did it said that it was okay, and that my mom said he can do it. I was just 8 years old and didn't know what I wanted to say or do to this man who was making me feel shame and taking my childhood away.

I went through court and they said that they had to throw the case out just for the simple fact that the case was in two different cities and that I waited too long to say something about it, and some other junk. I felt like they thought I was telling a lie. Now when I think about it, I wish that I never had told anyone because it makes me cry to think that they know what my mom's boyfriend did to me and my life, and I wish that he didn't even know me. Then maybe I could do things that I can't see myself doing now. And that's being a little girl but now it's too late. I'll never really get to be a little girl and I just feel like dying.

DAWN

This is an example of a typical day in Dawn's life.

Well, this whole weekend was a blast! I slept over Ashley's house and we got up at 7:00am to go to Saturday School, since we missed serving our detentions for skipping. We got on the bus at 7:20 on the DOT *(Department of Transit)* and we went to Mickey D's and ate a big meal and we saw Hailey across the street. We went outside and yelled to her and she came running across the street and she finished my breakfast. By that time it was 8:10 am and we left Mickey D's and we got to school at 8:19 am and a girl or a lady told us we were late. Then Mr. Sherman came up to us and we went outside and he said, "Why are you late?" and he was yelling at us and he said we have After School Detention for one hour. Then he said, "Better yet, you get suspension!" and we all started to say stuff to him and he said a whole lot of stuff and even called us names, and he told us to leave and if we did not leave there would be a cop waiting to take us to Juvenile Detention Center so we knew to keep our mouths shut. We walked away and we went all the way back to Mickey D's and waited for the city bus and me, Ashley and Hailey went to Ashley's house for 20 minutes. Then we walked all the way back to the bus stop and waited for 30 minutes and it finally came and we were on the way to the mall to go shopping. We were there for half of the day. It was fun. We ate a lot of food, went into almost every store, but we didn't buy nothing cuz we didn't bring any money.

SA'RINA

Her mom abandoned her and her dad worked two jobs.

Last night I don't remember anything because I took these CCD cold pills from Publix that made me get all messed up. It started when I went to Char's house at about 5:30 at night. Trevor, Dennis, and Alex were there. They said that they took some cold and cough pills too so they were messed up. Trevor took like 16 of them, Armando took like 9, and Char took 11. So we went to get some more at Publix. Char is really good at just walking in and stealing them. When we got back, I took 8. I didn't think that they were going to do anything. I thought they were just messing around. So I took them, and we left.

Nothing was happening at first, so then I really thought they were lying. About a half hour later, it started working. I don't remember much of what happened. Alex says that I kept passing out and I couldn't even walk. They said that they walked me home. When I woke up this morning, I had a bad headache. And I was really tired. I didn't remember anything.

I really hope that I didn't do anything bad because my dad seemed like he was mad at me when I wasn't home. I woke up this morning at my friend's house. I woke up at six o'clock. When I went home, everyone was awake. So I took quick shower, got dressed, ate a bowl of cereal, and I left and got on the city bus and went to school. Only thing is,

Char was on the same bus and he gave me 10 more pills, so I took them and went to school. Ms. Preuss noticed something was wrong, and they had the paramedics come and get me since my heart was going so fast. That was scary. Next time I won't take so many of them pills. I only think I'll take like 4, maybe.

SANDY

She had her healthy baby boy while she was my student.

If I could erase one event from my life I would erase the time I first smoked weed. The reason I would erase this is because when I first smoked, I liked it and I got so high that I did something really stupid. I took a car and crashed it into a light post, and my friends could of died or got hurt. I almost went to jail, but the owner of the car covered for me.

The other reason that I choose this event is because after that first time I smoked weed, I liked it and I kept doing it every chance I got and one time, I wanted it so bad that when my mom was sleeping, I went into her room and took $100 from her wallet. I used all the money for weed and then I started doing other drugs and I even started drinking and doing stuff that I should not have been doing. That is why if I could change any event in my life, I would change the first time I smoked weed and if I could change it, I would never smoke it. I swear.

ROLANDO

Rolando needed a father figure in his life, but only had his mom.

Well, I've done a lot of bad things. Some were too bad to say, but still, I'll tell you some of them. I'm pretty good at stealing, I mean you name it and I stole it, but I hate getting caught and that has only happened to me twice. Well, not including getting snitched on about Sammy's cell phone.

Like, I've been caught stealing from Sears. I took this set of flashlights that came with a free belt to hold the flashlights. I put the pack in my jacket and I walked out. The whole time I was praying for the alarm not to sound. So I walked out and nothing happened so I kept on walking.

This weird looking dude came up to me and without saying anything started to check my pockets. I thought he was some retard trying to mug me. So I pushed him away and stuck him in his nose. Blood splashed all over the floor and he started to yell, "ARE YOU STUPID, I'M A COP!!!"

He pulled out his badge and threw me to the ground. He took the flashlights and put cuffs on me. Everyone around me was staring at me. I was so embarrassed, my shirt had blood all over my back and neck cuz when the cop pinned me down, he was still dripping blood. He picked me up and I kicked him in his nuts and told him to get away from me. They brought me to the police station and arrested me for one day. They let me go cuz the cop forgot to read me my rights and didn't handle the situation the correct way. So I laughed in his bandaged face and went home.

HAILEY

Most of the time, she was trying to raise herself, but she seemed very happy to be doing so.

When I was twelve I moved to Beach Haven, Florida. My mom was having problems with her boyfriend, Doug. He wanted to get her smoking crack. She wouldn't, so he became close to my mom's and my friend, Jerry, who smokes crack a lot. My mom and him had been together five years so far. All of a sudden with the crack, Doug went crazy!

First, he started bringing this lady named Carla in my house when my mom was not there to smoke crack. So I told my mom and we moved four apartments over. Then one day, Doug started hanging out with a friend of my mom's and I. Doug started hanging out with Jerry so much. Jerry ended up letting Doug move into his other bedroom in his house with his wife and kids and be his roommate, like I used to be.

One night, my little brother and I went over to Jerry's to bake cookies. When I got halfway done making cookies, Carla was in Doug's room for a long time, but I did not know. She went to leave and on her way out she gave me a dirty look, then said something about my mom. I walked her to the door and when she walked out I yelled, "Crack Whore!" then slammed the door.

She turned around and came back inside and got in my face. Pointing her finger in my face. My brother held me away. I told her to get her finger out of my face and I gave her three chances. The fourth time she did it, I grabbed her head and hit it against the wall, then I punched her three times and said, "That's for talking about my mom, B****!"

She started crying. I said, "Wait, Ho, hold on, let me get my mom." So I went and woke up my mom in our apartment, and we went to Jerry's house. She was kind of mad but she was happy that I finally beat the b****'s ass for stealing her boyfriend. Carla had always been walking by my mom and starting sh**. So my mom laughed in her face, which looked pretty crappy where I hit her, and then we left, and we were laughing all the way home.

My mom was so glad I did it in a way, cuz if she would have done it, she would have went to jail because she is an adult and Carla is 33. So then me and my mom ate some cookies and went to sleep.

The next morning at 6am Carla was over at our place knocking at the door. My mom opened it, pushed her away, laughed cuz she really looked like shit with bruises, and slammed the door in her face. She wouldn't leave, and my mom and I were yelling for Carla to get her fat a** off our front door, but she would just keep yelling, so we called the cops, and when Carla saw them coming she ran away.

ASHLEY

Even though the odds were against her, she was hoping for a bright future.

When I get out of high school I plan to go to college. I have to stay in medical school for four years. After I go to school and pass all my classes, I'm going to be a doctor. The reason I want to be a doctor is because I would really enjoy helping people. I would really enjoy helping kids too. I really think I want to be a pediatrician. I want to be a pediatrician because I really, really love kids. They are our future. I have always wanted to work with kids. After I get out of high school then I'll go to college for my degree. My job is going to be very hard. You have to make the right choice all the time, never the wrong one, because you only have a little time to do things. If they are not done correctly then someone's life could be put in danger. The only thing I'm worried about is that I might make the wrong choice and someone could lose their life. A doctor is a very hard job.

* * *

CHAPTER EIGHT

SANDY

It was early Fall of that first year, when I was asked to take six additional students for just one day. One of the other DOP teachers was absent, the substitute had not showed up, and no other teacher could possibly handle these six super defiant kids. I already had a full class of my own so I wasn't exactly celebrating, but I understood the predicament the school was in and I agreed to do it. There were two boys, one black and one white, with hair to his waist in white boy dreads with lots of piercings, and four girls, one Hispanic, one white, two black. Sandy was dark skinned, full makeup and neatly dressed. I noticed her right away. She didn't look like the others. She wore a short denim skirt, and fitted white shirt, press on multicolored orange and purple nails with little diamonds separating the colors, and had long black braids in her hair with little white beads at the bottom of each.

I ran my class very differently than the other three DOP teachers. They had a military system of order, having kids do pushups, sit-ups, or some other physical punishment if they talked out of turn. It worked for them, but as a PE teacher for ten years, I would never think to ask kids to do exercise as a punishment. It went against everything I believed in. Exercise was not a punishment in my mind, but a reward. Do you punish a child by teaching them math or giving them a science assignment? Of course not!

Apparently, the other DOP teachers, all burly, strong, manly men, with loud voices, whose classes took up an entire wing at the back-end of our school, didn't agree with the way I did things, and sometimes told their students as much. As the lone female in the DOP mix, my unusual methods seemed to rub the other teachers the wrong way. They might have thought I was too "soft." Go figure! One thing's for sure… I'm almost certain they were surprised I had lasted as long as I had with my rowdy, difficult, volatile, yet lovable bunch! I do believe they had bets going on how long I'd last!

The DOP teacher I replaced also had more of a military, disciplinarian attitude himself. Not only had I been fully briefed by the students who had had him the year before, but I actually found a few crowbars wrapped in duct tape when I took over my class. I assume they were there to bring fear to the unruly troops. I even got a kick out of holding one in the air from time to time to remind my students what things could be like in DOP! But, being "soft" worked for me, as long as I was only soft about the things *I wanted* to be soft about, so it was just not going to change. My every step seemed to be guided by a force bigger than myself. I knew it from that first day. And, being with the same kids all day, you develop quite a bond. My bond could be a "soft" one if I wanted it to be.

I tried not to pay the military men any mind, and stay out of the other DOP teachers' business, but occasionally our students would intermingle, fight on campus, or have entanglements afterschool, so there was invariably friction that we had to keep in check at all times. Being professional amidst our differences was essential. I decided never to play the female card, but looking back, it might have been wise.

The six kids who came to me that day loved their teacher and respected him and his military style of keeping order, as much as my kids loved me with my mom-like, love-them-no matter-what, lets-work-this-out-as-a-family style. But, I'm relatively certain they had heard enough about me and my unusual ways to enter my room with caution and skepticism. I'm pretty sure, considering the sneers I perceived on some of their faces, these kids had it out for me from the moment they walked in. I'm also sure if their teacher had any idea the kids would be sent to me, he would have preferred to come to school rather than subject them to a day in my class.

Students had told me the other DOP teachers didn't really approve of my methods. But, the administrators, the parents, and the kids appreciated my way of handling things and that was what mattered to me. And I had to admit, they were very good at what they did, and I was very good at what I did. We all kept order of a potentially dangerous and difficult to control bunch, each in our own way, and we'll leave it at that for now.

Once the kids were seated, it didn't take long for something to erupt. I was able to contain the boys quickly, but the girls got loud and disrespectful to the point that the kids in my class wanted to fight them to shut them up. We came close to having an all out rumble in there, so I figured I had to act all mean and loud for a second to calm things down. Once I'd done that, and everyone had sat back down, the four girls were staring evil glares at me, they looked at me like they were plotting to *take me down*. I went back to teaching but soon enough the four girls began to make inappropriate comments.

I wasn't about to have them do push-ups or sit-ups or stand against a wall, or anything like that, so I calmly said, "Look, I'm just doing your teacher a favor. His sub didn't show up, and they had to split his class up. Nobody else can handle you, and nobody else would even try. You are stuck with me and I am stuck with you right now. Let's just make the best of it, shall we? If you don't want to learn anything, then just be quiet, so my students can learn."

"Look at her trying to act like she can give me orders," Sandy shot right back, laughing. My class was stunned. No one ever talked to me like that.

Latoya, one of my most beloved and loyal students, but one who definitely packed a punch and wasn't afraid to swing, jumped out of her seat and went to hit Sandy, fist clenched. "B*****, I'm a split you right here!" Kiko, jumped in front of her to stop her, and managed to push her back to her seat. The other kids just watched, throwing in a comment or two.

"It's okay, Latoya," Kiko said. "Don't get yourself in trouble over her. She's only here for one day."

Sandy just laughed, angering Latoya all the more, who yelled, "B*****, I'm a slap your face and pull your fancy weave out your hair!" Kiko could hardly hold her; her arms were flailing to reach Sandy. Ghost got up to help Kiko get her settled down, and back to her seat.

While that was still going on, Ashley yelled from the other side of the room. "Don't talk like that to my teacher again or I'll ram my fist down your throat, and there's nobody in this room will stop it! Them boys can't stop me, like they did her!"

Great, all I needed now was for Ashley and Latoya to get into one of their customary brawls and all hell would break loose in my room. But I remained calm. *I don't know how! But somehow I remained calm!*

Sandy stood up, brushing her long braids behind her shoulders, then putting both hands in the air, motioning for Ashley to come closer, and doing one of those little circular spins with her neck, she said, "Come and try it, b****!!!"

Before Ashley could get up, or Latoya bounced to her feet again, I stood right in front of Sandy. Clearly, Latoya and Ashley were putting their differences aside for a moment to join forces against the rude intruder to our usually quiet class. I knew this could unravel into violence, and that was the last thing I wanted. Sandy acted like a fighter, but she didn't look like one. That hair of hers would definitely be the first thing Latoya or Ashley would rip from her head and leave in bits on the ground. I didn't want to see that. She looked so pretty. What was she so angry about?

Things had been relatively peaceful in my class since I had taken over. I didn't have too much of the typical in-class fighting DOP had been known for. I also didn't want to call for security to come and help me, because that would show the students that I needed help to control things, and I wasn't about to show that kind of weakness with this volatile bunch. I stood right next to Sandy, made no eye contact, and said, "Sit down," in the calmest, most direct tone possible. I said it as if I actually expected her to sit.

She hesitated a minute, so I inched closer and said it again, more slowly and deliberately, pointing my gaze at the desk where I wanted her body to get back to. I knew I couldn't turn my back to Ashley, or Latoya, until I had Sandy under control and in her seat, but there was a second there that I wondered if Ashley or Latoya would come around me and pounce on Sandy anyway.

I was pleasantly surprised when Sandy finally sat down. She probably didn't really want to fight Ashley. Everyone knew Ashley could fight, and everyone knew that everyone she'd fought, male and female alike on campus, ended up in the emergency room. The whole school knew that, surely these kids knew it. And although Latoya hadn't earned as feared a reputation, she was big, she was loud, and she could fight. I was certain Sandy only wanted to show off for her classmates, so I thought I'd go ahead and let her show her force just a bit. She was a big girl, and tall. Mean looking, I guess, if you could look past, the fancy clothes, the fingernails, and the weave.

My instinct to tell her to sit, without making eye contact, was right on. It seemed like a primal move in some ways, an instinct that came from deep inside me. But, she was quiet and back in her seat. The fight had been diffused.

I had almost regained my composure, and gone back to the lesson, when another one of the visiting students said, "Sandy, you gonna let that lady tell you what to do?"

Sandy then shot out of her seat and said, "Whatever, man, I'm out of here," and she sashayed herself out.

I watched her go and slam the door behind her. "Anyone else want to join her? This is your time to go. Right now then... go on out the door," I said. Two of the three other girls went with her.

I called the office to tell Ms. Rodriguez they were probably on their way to her, and I continued on with my lesson. The two boys and the girl who were left were no trouble at all after that.

An hour later, Ms. Rodriguez came back to my room with Sandy and one other girl. By then we were doing Science, and I had some supplies out on all the kids' desks.

"Ms. Preuss, I had one of the girls sent home, and these two have been in my office since lunch. I've spoken to them, and they promise there will be no more outbursts. Will you please take them back?" I knew no one else could handle them, and that they'd most probably made the last hour a living hell for the office staff. I really liked Ms. Rodriguez. I wanted to help her. I nodded with a bit of hesitation.

I pointed out two desks in a corner of the room and told Ms. Rodriguez they could both sit there till the end of the day, on one condition: they would have to apologize to me and my class for disrupting instruction.

The first girl apologized immediately, "I'm sorry for being disrespectful," she said to the class. She seemed contrite, and I pointed to the desk where she could sit. She went over and sat in it.

Now Sandy stood there next to Ms. Rodriquez. She took a look at me, at Ashley, at Latoya and said, with a smirk on her face, "I changed my mind, I don't want to be here, and I ain't saying no apology to nobody. You can give me a referral. I don't care." She turned and walked out the door.

"I'm very sorry, Ms. Preuss," Ms. Rodriguez said. "I appreciate what you've done today. There's no excuse for the way Sandy is behaving."

"It's alright, she doesn't know me. I know how it is."

Ms. Rodriguez left and I finished the day with the four students from the other DOP class without incident. I think by the end of the day they came away with the feeling that my class wasn't so terrible after all. We had an interesting science lab and all my students, including our guests, were inquisitive and respectful, and interested in the lesson. I think they might have been surprised at how nicely things ran.

From time to time after that, I would see Sandy in the hall. She would never say hello, although the other four who had spent the day with me would wave and smile-- but not Sandy. She never acknowledged me, ever.

Then one day, many weeks later, I noticed her at the other end of the hall with what looked like a baby bump. She would give me dismissive looks and go on about her business. She never spoke to me, or smiled. Clearly her day with me was still a wedge between us.

I also felt it. I was usually able to bring kids around in a relatively short period of time. I was surprised I had never been able to reach Sandy. She was such a pretty girl, confident in her stride. Her black skin was smooth, contrasted nicely with her light colored eyes. She liked dressing up more than most of the other girls in DOP, and every day she wore those light brown contact lenses in her eyes. I could tell she was making an effort to always look her best. Didn't smile much, though.

She had been somewhat of an enigma, someone I couldn't understand. As she walked about with her small baby bump, I figured I never would understand her. I wasn't close enough to her to talk to her about it, so I just watched from afar as her stomach grew a little at a time, and the rumors finally began to swirl.

At one point the possibility of her pregnancy became a topic of side bar conversation in my classroom. Most of the students who heard were amazed and astounded. To their knowledge, no one had ever attended Destiny Middle

School while pregnant. I heard she didn't even know she was pregnant when I first saw her baby bump. I heard it was only a few weeks ago that she had realized, and she wasn't saying much. No one knew who the father was. She hadn't been going out with anyone. No one knew anything, not even her teacher.

I found it difficult to believe her teacher hadn't noticed, but he was a man. It might have escaped him. When I'd seen the bump, I never told anyone, I figured it would get to me eventually, and it did. What surprised me is that she had kept this secret to herself and just a few people in her class and some of the other girls in DOP. No counselor knew. No administrator. Her parents didn't know. No one.

The little bump was easy enough to cover, with a jacket or loose fitting blouse, but as it swelled, it was harder and harder for me to understand why nothing had been done. When I heard my students talking, they affirmed they were hearing the rumor, but that she didn't want anyone to know. Having been placed in foster care just a year before, said she didn't want her foster parents to find out and that she didn't want to get kicked out of school.

"Her mom's in jail and doesn't want her. Her foster parents are really good to her. She gets spoiled over there. She never dressed up nice last year. I think she wants them to adopt her for good." Dawn confided. "If she gets pregnant, maybe they take her out of there or something. I don't know, Miss. But she looks pregnant to me."

I also heard there was a rumor that it was a boy in her class who had gotten her pregnant, but no one knew which boy it was. If I'd had a closer relationship with her teacher, I might have approached him, but I didn't think it was a good idea, so I just stayed out of it completely. My heart broke for her, but she wasn't going to be able to ignore the pregnancy, if it was a pregnancy, for long!

Being in my first year of teaching an at-risk DOP population run within a regular school, where regular classes were still functioning, I found this to be fascinating. When I taught at Somerset Alternative School in Los Angeles, the whole school was geared toward Drop-Out Prevention. There was an entire class there for pregnant girls. In fact, I'd often substitute taught there and had to show the girls how to carry a baby, change diapers, etc. There, the entire school was DOP. They were even allowed smoke cigarettes in the courtyard during class breaks. But to see a young girl walking around the halls of Destiny Middle School with a baby bump hiding under her blouse was quite something.

Since I had no relationship with her and didn't feel that she wanted one, and I wasn't her teacher, nor did I hold any official charge over her, I decided to mind my own business. I took what the students said as hearsay, rumors and fantasy fiction, which I often had to do to keep my sanity. It was the only way I could wrap my brain around ignoring Sandy, and I managed to do it a few more weeks.

Then one day in late November, Mr. Spitzer showed up at my door, as he often did when he wanted to beg me to take a student into my class. He would come over, all 6'8" of him, head held low as he knocked at my door, smiling that guilty smile, his black skin glistening as the Florida sun will make skin do. This was his usual M.O. when he wanted to give me a heart-felt pitch about why a student might benefit from the inclusion into my class. He was hard to resist. I knew he had good intentions. I also trusted him enough to know he wouldn't bring me a student unless he really felt the kid needed to be in my class, and that it would be a good fit all around. He was somewhat genius in that respect. He understood people. He understood me.

I always thought it was very respectful how he would come by and ask if I would take, "just one more student." (One year I actually had 32 in my class!) Usually, I would give him a run for his money, make him sweat, but in the end I always said yes. In another county, where I'd also taught in an at-risk setting, there was no asking politely if you'd take a student, no knock on the door. The kid would just appear with papers in his hand and you had not one say about how you did or didn't like it. So, on one sunny day when he showed up with Sandy, I took my time to listen respectfully to his plea. He didn't really know about the history with us the day she was in my class, so I just listened.

Sandy stood off to the side about 10 feet away from where Mr. Spitzer and I huddled at the door. She looked like she didn't want to be there with him. My class was inside working on a writing assignment, but they could see through the glass windows, as usual.

"You see, Ms. Preuss, I have a problem. I need to get this girl out of the other DOP class right away. There's a boy in there she doesn't get along with. And I can't put her back in regular classes."

"Really? Why? Why can't you put her back in regular classes?" I said. Of course I knew the answer, but I wanted to hear it from his own lips, so I continued. "She looks like a nice young girl." I made sure to look her up and down and say that loud enough for her to hear it.

His eyes seemed to plead with me, he looked over to her, then back at me, "Ms. Preuss, she swears like a sailor, and not just at the kids either. She ripped her teachers apart all last year, that's why we had to put her in the DOP program."

"Hmmmm. Does she swear in her class now?" I knew the answer to that too. I heard her tell her teacher to "F" off a week ago when he yelled at her, then she'd turned around and given him the finger as she walked herself to the office. Usually no one gave her teacher the finger, most kids were too afraid to, so I knew she had some bite to her.

"Well, Ms. Preuss, you know, none of these kids are Saints, but Sandy isn't as bad as some of the others." He said, shrugging his shoulders. "She really needs to get out of there. She fought this boy twice already."

"So, Sandy is a fighter, and she will even fight boys," I said more to Sandy than to Mr. Spitzer, "You know she doesn't much like me," I said, trying to get her to make eye contact, but she just looked down at her feet, with both her hands tucked into her red jacket, and acted like she couldn't hear. "She was in here one day, and it didn't work out... isn't that right, Sandy?" I said directly at her, trying to coax her into the conversation.

She looked at me like she wanted to kill me. Mr. Spitzer looked surprised. Guess he hadn't heard about the day I had to watch Sandy. "She was here with a couple others, and how can I put it? We didn't quite get along."

"You don't like Ms. Preuss?" He asked Sandy, who just shrugged her shoulders. He gave her a stern look. One thing I knew about Mr. Spitzer is that he was full of surprises. He had the most unusual ways of handling problems, but he sure handled them. "Sandy, get over here."

She approached us, but didn't look one bit happy about it. "You let me come over here and bring you to Ms. Preuss' class without telling me about this?" He looked at her, hovering over her. "Well, do you want to be in her class or not? Because if you can't get along with Ms. Preuss, I don't know what to tell you. She's probably the easiest teacher in this school to get along with."

"She got in my face, and I don't like nobody in my face," she said, looking at her feet.

"Well," he said, nearing his face ever so close to hers, "You are going to get along with Ms. Preuss, or you are going to get kicked out of Destiny Middle School. Her class is, 'The Last Chance Motel' for you. Do you know what that means?"

Sandy shrugged her shoulders defiantly.

Mr. Spitzer continued. "That means that if you don't find a way to stay here, there's a long road ahead of you, and no place else to go. I won't put you back in regular classes. Maybe I'll have you expelled. But that could take a while, and you'd have to stay in the class you are in."

"I can't stay in there no more," she interrupted him. "Me and Roger got beef."

"I could send you to an alternative school, or I can have your foster parents withdraw you from school and home school you. That's it. Those are your only choices."

"No, don't do that! I want to stay here and go to a regular high school. I want to graduate from regular high school." She yelled it at him; I saw the desperation in her face. She wanted to get an education. She meant it.

"Looks like you'll have to learn to get along with Ms. Preuss then!" he yelled back.

She bit her lips and crossed her arms, and yelled at him again, "Fine, I'll be in her class!"

I finally had to break into this compelling interaction. I was so shocked that she yelled at Mr. Spitzer, and that he'd allowed it! He wasn't one to let something like that go, but then again, perhaps her being a girl played into it. Perhaps he already knew she was pregnant and hadn't told me yet.

Perhaps he felt sorry for her because she had to be placed in foster care last year when her mother went to jail. I wasn't sure, but I had a few things of my own to interject, so I busted in right after she yelled her agreement to be in my class.

I looked her right in her light brown contact lens colored eye… "This is all very interesting to me, but I haven't said I'd take you yet."

"You see!" She yelled back at Mr. Spitzer, "She wants to get in my face again."

"Ms. Preuss wasn't getting in your face," Mr. Spitzer yelled.

I put my hand on her shoulder. I knew that was a risk, but it was one I had to take. I was surprised when she neither flicked my hand off with her own, nor pulled her shoulder back as if to say 'don't you touch me' with her body language. Instead, she looked in my eyes. It was almost as if my hand had a calming effect on her. She might have been surprised I was willing or daring enough to touch her, who knows what she was thinking. My hand seemed to know it needed to be on her shoulder. All I know is I had her looking at me softly, and that was just what I needed.

"Sweetie," I said, as earnestly and calmly as I could, "I know you are heated, and it can't be easy to have to change classes, and it looks as if you and Mr. Spitzer aren't getting along all that well either, but… this isn't me trying to get in your face. Believe me, the day I get in your face, I'll be yelling up a storm. This is my trying to make this a win-win situation. We both need to win here."

Of course, I had to throw in a little Steven Covey doctrine her way. He'd been my professor at Brigham Young University, after all, and was now a famous author! His win-win boardroom theories had worked many a time in my classroom. *It has to be win-win, or you have to walk away.*

She gave me this look like I was crazy, which of course, most of the kids know I am to some degree or another, or I wouldn't be able to work with them as well as I do. Mr. Spitzer knew to stay out of it. And I kept my voice calm, my hand on her shoulder, and my eyes looking into hers.

"That's right. We both have to win, and we have some unfinished business, you and I." She stared me down and I did the same in return. She didn't respond right away, so I continued... "The last day you were here, you were given the opportunity to stay in my class. All you had to do was apologize to me and my class for the disruption you created. You didn't want to do that, so you weren't allowed to stay. Now you want to come in. You *need* to come in because you and Roger 'got beef' right?"

She shook her head, and listened intently, with a quizzical look on her face as I went on... "So you want me to be your teacher now, and that means I'll have to respect you and you'll have to respect me. That's how it works in my class. But we got off to a rocky start didn't we?"

Suddenly, she looked different. Not just quiet, but humble. The change was palpable. Her eyes welled up a bit, and her glossy lips quivered as she answered, "Yeah. It was a messed up way to start off."

"Okay," I went on, so here's the deal. First I need to know why you and Roger aren't getting along.

"He keeps talking crap about me, and I don't like it."

"So he talks 'crap' and you don't like it and then... what... you hit him?" I find that using their language right back at them is helpful. I usually never do it in front of another educator because I know they wouldn't understand, but Mr. Spitzer understands because he does the same thing when he needs to. He will say things in the way the kid needs to hear it, that's part of his magic, so I went ahead and spoke as freely as I felt I needed to speak in order to reach her.

"Well, you know what… People will talk 'crap' all day long, and if you hit every one who talks crap, you will be in jail. In fact, so will I. See Mr. Spitzer here, he talks crap all the time. Sometimes, right at me, and I can't go off and hit him just because I want to, now can I? In fact, I'd like to hit him right now because he's here at my door when I need to be teaching my classes, bringing me a student I have no room for. So if I could hit him, I would. But I'm not hitting him, am I? And you know what… hearing me say that, he might want to hit me right now too. Did you ever think of that? Did you ever think that teachers are walking around this school wanting to hit each other?" She opened her eyes wide and shook her head, "But we can't do that because a) it's wrong, and b) we would go to jail. So if we can't do it, neither can you."

"You really want to hit Mr. Spitzer? Cuz I want to hit him too!"

"Yeah, I really, really want to hit him some times. That man right there can be aggravating!"

She smiled, and looked at Mr. Spitzer who was smiling too, and shaking his head. I looked at Mr. Spitzer, "Tell her the truth, don't you want to hit people sometimes too?" And he's not the only one either. Teachers all over this school do things to upset each other all the time. We can't all go around hitting each other. And guess what? Sometimes we get upset at the Principal too. We just can't hit people who upset us. We'd go to jail for that. For kids hitting other kids, the punishment is usually ten days suspension. For adults, it's assault and battery charges, a trial that costs lots of money, and then time in jail. Hitting people isn't a joke, and I'll expect you to settle that part of yourself if you are going to be in my class."

"I only ever fought this year with Roger. I don't fight for just no reason."

"Well that's good to hear, but I do recall you wanting to fight a certain young lady in my class not so long ago. And... what is it about this 'crap' Roger talks about that upsets you so much that you lose control and you hit him?"

She looked hesitantly at Mr. Spitzer, and clenched her teeth. "I don't want to talk in front of that man no more." Tears welled up in her eyes, and started down her cheeks as she said that.

I sensed that there was a big back story, perhaps the one the kids had rumored about, or something about her foster home status that Mr. Spitzer knew about that I didn't. I sensed I wasn't going to be able to uncover it right there outside my door in the afternoon sun, so I moved on. "Well, you and I can sort all of that out as time goes on if you are in my class. It's still a big if."

"Mr. Spitzer," I said, "I think Sandy and I are starting to communicate now. I have a feeling we can work this out. So here's the thing," I said, turning back to Sandy. "The point is that you have yet to apologize to me and my class for your outburst and behavior the day you were here. And as far as "beef" goes, well you have some of that in my class going on with a few of my students, don't you?"

She was moving between gazing into my eyes hoping to beg her forgiveness, and looking down at her feet in embarrassment, so I continued, "Now, I know you may not be used to apologizing, but my class knows that apologizing is important to me, so they do it. Do you think you can go in there and apologize?"

She looked stunned. She was speechless. I removed my hand from her shoulder, where it had rested for a very long time, and took a step back. "That's your ticket into my classroom," I said, and tilted my head towards the door.

Mr. Spitzer stood there silently for a moment, and watched as she looked hesitant and thoughtful, clearly evaluating all the ramifications to her ego if she went in my class and had to apologize after she had left in a huff a few weeks before feeling triumphant.

"So here's how it will be. You can leave now and go wherever you end up with Mr. Spitzer, or you can apologize as I asked you to do that day. That's my win-win offer. Take it or leave it?"

"I'm not going to go anywhere with him," she almost growled, shifting her eyes his way a bit.

"Very well then," I said. "The choice has been made. Mr. Spitzer, go ahead and leave her here, and as soon as she is ready to do what she needs to do for me, she will be allowed to be in my class."

"Ms. Preuss, you sure now?" Mr. Spitzer said, looking a bit worried for me. I looked at Sandy's eyes and saw a new softness in them that even her fancy colored contact lenses couldn't hide. I knew she was between a rock and a hard place. I knew she wanted to be able to stay in my class, so I knew she *wanted* to apologize, but it was a struggle for her to do so. I decided I'd do whatever it took to make it easy for her to apologize. Getting Mr. Spitzer out of the picture was part of helping that to happen.

"I'm sure," I said to him. "I'm going to give her some time. If she hasn't come around by lunch time, I'll send her to your office and you can do whatever you need to do with her, but I have a feeling we'll work it out."

"Ok then, I'll be in my office and I'll check with you at lunch." He looked over to Sandy. "This really is your last chance. Nobody but Ms. Preuss would dance this dance with you and give you all this time to make amends. I have no problem booting you out of this school, so you better get along with Ms. Preuss or I'll be back to yank you out of here!"

She turned her head and face away from him as he spoke, wanting to try to ignore him. It was my game now. And I couldn't afford to let his words or any animosity between he and Sandy cause her to explode right there in front of him and spoil the last few minutes we had worked so hard to create. So rather than let her answer him, or let him go on speaking and possibly igniting a fuse in her, I ignored him altogether and spoke directly to her.

"Sandy, I know you are going to do the right thing. So, you can stand out here and think this through as long as you need. You can go to the bathroom and pull yourself together. I can even bring a chair out here and you can sit for a while if you like, but when you open the door to my classroom, and I let you walk in, you will be apologizing to me and to the entire class. Do you understand?"

"Yes," was all she said, and shook her head up and down and wiped her tears off with her fingers.

"Go ahead, go to the bathroom if you need, wash the tears off your face, get your make up back on nice and pretty." I opened the door to my class. "Danny, do me a favor and bring me a chair out here. We might be getting a new student." I winked at her as she walked off to the bathroom, and Mr. Spitzer made his way towards the office, with his tall, lanky, long legged self and huge uneven steps.

When I came back in the class, the journal writing time was over. They were usually quiet when these sorts of things went down outside of my classroom, as they sometimes did, right outside of those big windows, partly because they wanted to try to eavesdrop and partly because they knew if I had to open the door to discipline them, the rest of the day could go sour. I have a great sense of humor as an educator, and the kids know it. But, there's this other side to me, and one thing I am usually able to accomplish within the first few weeks of school is to go off on someone in a way that makes everyone else want to never have me go off on them again. I call it turning into a "Middle-Aged Cuban Woman."

I let my hot, Cuban temper show through, *usually* pure theatrical posturing, and I make sure my comments have as much of a return bite as I get. I can come right up to the line of what's appropriate without passing it. I can say just enough to make them wish they hadn't tangled with me. It's really funny, sort of a gift. Just call me the teen whisperer... I speak their language, I somehow penetrate into their heads. I can get the whole class laughing, while the one kid I am reprimanding feels uncomfortable, even slightly scalded, but in a way that he learns, and understands his actions. I don't plan it. Stuff just starts coming out of my mouth and oddly enough, it's just the right stuff. Seriously, it comes from somewhere up above. I can't come up with that kind of crazy talk on my own! The benefit is that kids learn their lesson, and I don't have to write many referrals or call the office in on much. Everybody's happy.

In those moments when they are all quiet, I like to entertain the thought that the assignment I gave them was to their liking and that they respected me so much that they wanted to honor the fact that I'd asked them to be quiet while I dealt with something. I'm not sure why it was so. But it was so. Whenever I was outside that door by the windows, they were on task and they made me proud. It was not something they did naturally. I knew it was an effort for them, and one I very much appreciated. It had been this way since the very first days when Kyle and I would step out there. Then after I had found marijuana on him, they knew that interesting stuff goes down outside those windows, and they always kept quiet and in their seats, year after year, it was the same.

When I walked back in, I thanked them, and explained everything that went on. I let them know that Sandy would be our new student if she apologized.

"She ain't apologizing, Miss," Tony blurted out, but I ignored it, and we went on with our classes for about an hour. Sandy sat outside in an orange plastic chair for most of that time. It was both odd and touching to see this bucking bronco of a girl sit quietly in that chair, composing her thoughts, planning her apology. I knew she'd come in eventually. I just knew it. So I waited patiently until she was ready. When she finally opened the door, she just stood there with a blank look on her face.

"Well," I said, "Hi Sandy. Class, you guys remember Sandy? Mr. Spitzer wants her to be in our class now, and I agreed to let her. Sandy has something she wants to say to us." My whole demeanor was intended to alleviate tension. Of course they all remembered Sandy. And everyone knew just what she was about to do.

Sandy sort of smiled, "I'm sorry, Ms. Preuss." She said. Everyone in the class broke out in applause. This surprised Sandy and made her smile even more.

"What is it you are sorry for Sandy?" I always like to hear the kids verbalize exactly what they think they did wrong, otherwise to me, apologies are meaningless.

"I'm sorry I was disrespectful and disrupted your class."

"Thank you so much, Sandy," I said, "I accept your apology. Did you have something to say to the class?"

She looked around at all the kids and mustered the courage to say, "I'm sorry I dissed your teacher."

Again everyone applauded.

"Do you guys accept her apology? Are we all good now?" I asked.

Sandy looked around a bit puzzled, as the kids nodded and said, "Yes," in their various forms. I pointed around and said, "Pick an empty seat where you would like to sit," and she did.

"Okay guys, what Sandy just did was not easy for her to do. I accept her apology and I know you do too, so she's one of us now." Almost everyone was smiling. "We're on page 107 in the Geography book. Reach under your desk and grab it, Sandy." She reached, she grabbed, she opened the book, and she listened quietly to the lesson about the Inca Indians, then she did the assignment.

And that was that. Sandy was mine.

We went on with the lesson and I acted as if nothing particularly unusual had happened. When we walked to lunch, she walked quietly in my lunch line, like all the others. I left them at lunch as I always did, and by the time I picked them up, she had bonded in the ways she needed to bond with the class.

The afternoon was very nice and I realized that Sandy was very, very bright and loved to learn. School was important to her. The fact that she was still hiding a supposed baby bump was an issue I wasn't ready to deal with just yet.

I did, however, have a nice heart-to-heart talk with her at the end of the day, when the others had all gone home.

"I'm glad you apologized. It's not easy to do what you did. I think you and I are going to get along just fine, and everyone in the class seems to like you."

"Yeah," she said, "Apologizing wasn't as hard as I thought. It felt kinda good, actually. Me and Ashley and Latoya are straight now. We talked at lunch."

"See…there's a method to my madness."

"What does that mean?" she asked.

"It means that even though you may not understand why I am doing something--even if it looks like I am out of my mind, which I might even be from time to time--there's a reason I do what I do. There's a purpose to the steps I take. 'Method to my Madness'."

"Oh! I get it!"

"I'm sure you'll get me more and more as time goes on. And by the way, whenever you are ready to talk about Roger, you let me know."

I was also curious to know what could have resulted in a student needing to leave one DOP class to come to another. That hadn't happened before. I had gotten kids from other teachers in regular classes who were difficult to manage, but never from another DOP class. We all pretty much 'managed' our own.

"I can tell you about Roger," she said. "He's telling everybody I slept with him, but I didn't. He told the whole class. He was acting real proud about it too, so I fought him twice."

"That's not a nice thing for a guy to do, but they do it sometimes, don't they?"

"Yeah." She said and looked down.

"I can understand why you would want to hit him. But you have to know there are other ways of dealing with things." She just shook her head. I knew if I said the right things I could gain her trust and she would open up, even more than she already had. I knew it was vital that I do so. I still didn't know what she was going to do about her rumored baby, or if there even was a baby for sure. I just knew instinctively she *had* to trust me.

"Now that you're in my class, he won't be able to see you at school, and neither will the others from your old class. But if he tries to bother you again, if any of them bother you again, you let me know. I can take care of things, you know. I have my ways," I smiled softly as I said that, and lifted one brow.

"What do you mean?" she asked.

"It's hard to explain, but just trust me. I have unusual ways of making sure things get done." She stared deeply into my eyes. "If someone, anyone, is bothering you or saying things you don't like, I'm really, really good at making it stop. I'm slick about how I do it too, so they never know you told me."

I thought about the countless times I had gone behind the scenes during my career, pulling strings to make things happen. I knew how to stop rumors, bullying, anything really. It's like a gift. I just gather all the information and then I sort of create or allow a scenario whereby I can address the issue directly with the culprit as he's doing it. It works like magic. No one ever knows how I found out. They think I'm a mind reader, or a psychic.

"Okay, I'll let you know," she said, with a little smile and a twinkle of hope in her eyes. I knew then, that I had broken through, that I was beginning to reach the girl who needed love. I was happy because in the end, that's what they all need is love and understanding, someone to talk to them and listen, someone to really hear what they have to say. That would have been enough satisfaction for me, but then she did something that stunned me as much as it pleased me. She just looked at me like she was seeing me for the first time, and then she hugged me, and walked out the door.

As I watched her walk off at the end of that day through the very windows she had stood in front of and yelled, I felt like I was doing something important. I knew that what I had just pulled off there was not something every teacher could pull off. In less than one day, I had gained her trust and her affection.

What was different about me? Nothing really, except that for the first time in my career I had a commodity I had never been given before. I had time. Time to talk to kids who needed me; time to fully deal with issues as they presented themselves; time to let emotions run their course. I had time. I spent the entire day with the same kids. That's usually unheard of in middle school, and I believe this is why middle school is when we sometimes lose adolescents in the shuffle. They go from elementary school, where they have one teacher all day, to six different personalities, one each hour, in middle school.

In a normal classroom I would never have had that kind of *time*. I would have been too busy following my lesson plans to talk outside that door to Mr. Spitzer and Sandy. I would have been too involved in teaching to go through all the steps to get where I needed to be with that one kid.

Sandy would have fallen through the cracks. My class would never have learned a vital lesson about apologies, forgiveness, and putting one's ego aside. Sandy would never have known the curing power of an apology. I would never have known what a sweet child she was at the heart. She would never have known I wasn't so bad after all.

I was happy to be teaching these children who need so much. She walked out, and all these thoughts came over me as her frame grew small in the distance of the hallway. I was doing something that mattered--something that mattered very, very much. It wasn't about Science or Math or Geography. It was bigger than that. What my students needed was love and understanding, and someone to accept them. I wanted to devote myself to that end for Sandy and for all of them.

I knew from that moment on that teaching the lesson in my lesson plan was going to be secondary to teaching the lesson of life. I made the decision then and there, that reaching a child in a moment of need was more important to me and my class than finishing a "lesson" for the sake of the lesson itself. Once I made that transition in my mind, the rest came easily to me, like water flowing downstream. All the answers just came to me. The things I needed to say and do were given to me like gifts, one after the other, for years to come.

I'd sort of known that from the very first day, but I had to make the transition in my educator's mind. I had to accept that it was okay for me to do that, that I could allow myself to be a human being first and a teacher second, that I was going to let myself be guided by a higher source than the School Board of Sunshine County. That afternoon, I was able to figuratively throw away my lesson plans forever. I knew that I had a bigger purpose and that that purpose would direct my lessons and my heart forevermore.

I'll always thank Sandy for that. It's because of her that I began to look at my teaching in a different way. I became more confident in listening to my inner voice when it came to my students and my teaching. I had something to give and they needed what I had. I couldn't explain it, but I felt it. I just knew I was on the verge of something wonderful happening to me as a human being. It was a good feeling, and one that led to many changes in how I saw the world, and therefore in how I taught its citizens, my students.

* * *

About a month after Sandy came into my class, a few months pregnant by now, Sandy was still not confiding in me, but was fitting right in to my class. We got close very quickly. I'd never had a pregnant student before and wasn't sure what my role should be, if any. Perhaps her foster family was dealing with it privately and was planning an abortion? Perhaps the courts were involved? Perhaps Sandy was in denial? Perhaps her foster parents just hadn't noticed? I had no way to know the answers to those questions. But, I knew the instant she became my student, that it would be an issue for me to deal with, one way, or another.

I often tried to embrace her in conversation, hoping that she'd reveal it to me, but I didn't think it was my place to ask her directly so soon, and I wasn't sure if the office already knew. Perhaps she was only keeping her secret from me?

One day, just before Christmas, I thought it would be a good idea if the girls would help me wrap Christmas candles and potpourri I'd bought for the office staff. I brought in gold sheer fabric and gold lace. We sat at a big, kidney-shaped table I kept in the back of my room and we wrapped all the gifts one day after school. Sandy stayed longer than the others. I could tell she had something to get off her chest. I held my breath. I had known this moment would come.

"Miss," she said, slowly. "I think I'm pregnant."

I felt like a load was lifted from my shoulders. I had been on the verge of taking some sort of action, and was going to do so soon if she hadn't come forward herself.

Not only did she admit to me that she was pregnant. But I was surprised to find out it was Roger's baby.

"The Roger you've been fighting?" I gasped.

She nodded. "No one knows. My new mom don't know. Roger don't know. One day we was getting high and he made me have sex with him, then he's going around and saying I'm a ho, and booty loose and junk like that just because I don't want to go with him no more. I told him he had to leave me be."

My heart sank. She was not only pregnant, but had had all out fistfights in her old class with the father of her child while she was pregnant. I couldn't even begin to imagine what something like this felt like. Bewildered, I tried to gather my thoughts. I'd thought she might have had a boyfriend the family knew of, anything other than this glaring, bold, and difficult truth.

"If my foster daddy finds out he'll kill Roger."

I was stunned. "How does your foster daddy know Roger?" I had to ask.

She sat down in my big rolling desk chair, and straightened her skirt, hesitating. "Before I got in this foster home, I would hang with Roger, but when my mom had went to jail, I got these nice foster parents. They treat me right. I never had a place like this to live. It's a real house, with a yard, and flowers up front, and they said they want to adopt me. Me and my foster mom get on really good." She stopped for a second and I thought that was it. I thought I'd lost her. She looked at her fingernails, which were red and green for the holidays with little white flowers air brushed on the side. She was beginning to look emotional, her eyes tearing up. "We go get our hair and our nails done together, like a real mom and daughter. She really talks to me like she cares. She buys me the nicest clothes, and we laugh. We laugh so much. She never had a teenage girl as a foster kid before, and she really loves me like her own. It's like I'm part of a real family."

It was as if she was holding on to her only hope for a bright future. She stopped abruptly and got up and walked around to the other side of the table. "Oh, Miss, please don't tell this to nobody, or the courts will get real mad." She said, almost begging.

"Of course not. I won't tell anyone anything you tell me yourself in confidence without your permission. I felt like I was on the edge of a precipice, about to drop.

She looked so embarrassed suddenly, as if what she'd already told me wasn't enough. What more could there be? She took a deep breath, and so did I. "They don't like white people much and they didn't want me to see Roger since I got there. They told me as soon as they took me in it had to stop. I can't even have any white friends over! Miss, my mom had me when she was 15, and never went back to school. I don't want to end up like that. I want to do whatever they tell me to do. If they don't like white people, I don't need to like white people either, and I sure don't need to be with no Roger."

"So what are you going to do?"

"I don't know." She cast her eyes downward.

"Who have you told?" I asked.

"Just a few of my friends."

"I'm glad you told me. I sort of knew it already. Well, I didn't know it was Roger, but I saw a belly growing, and the kids were talking about it, but I didn't want to believe it was true."

"You never told on me," she said, eyes wide with surprise.

"How could I tell on you when I never heard it from your own lips? I thought and hoped it was just a rumor." I didn't want to tell her that I had hoped her foster family knew and was taking care of it somehow. I mean, how could they not see her body changing? How did I see it and not them? She must have been hiding her secret very guardedly at home.

"What about your real mom? Does she know?"

"My mom is a crack head. My mom never cared about me. I most always lived with my grandmother. They told her after my grandmother died last year that if she went back to jail one more time, they'd take me away from her. She don't care. I don't have anybody. She got herself juiced up on something and caught selling to an undercover. She never loved anything but drugs from the day I was born, maybe even before." She held her chin up high as she spoke about her real mom, like it was something she wanted to show herself she was over.

"It takes a lot of courage to tell me this," I continued, "but now we are going to have to do something about it."

She took a deep breath. "I know."

"Are you ready to do what you need to do?" She just shrugged. "This won't be easy. We are going to have to tell your foster mom. The school will need to know."

She took a deep breath and nodded her head. "She's gonna die, Miss. I don't want her to know. That lady is my like my mom now, like my grandmother was to me. I can't lose her. She will be so hurt if she finds out Roger is my baby's daddy. She made me promise I wasn't going to hang out with him anymore, and I betrayed her. I love her, Miss. I really do love her."

That was the first time I'd heard that term. 'My baby's daddy,' or 'My baby daddy' as they say nowadays would come to be a common term to me as each and every year I taught Drop-Out Prevention, I had at least one pregnancy to deal with, and sometimes two.

"How long have you known?" I asked Sandy.

"I haven't had my period since summer." I did the math and was floored. She looked no more than two months pregnant. If it happened over the summer she would be four to six months pregnant: too late for an abortion.

I held her hand and told her we'd do this together. We both walked down the corridor, and through the office. Sandy seemed timid and small to me for the first time. We went in to Mr. Spitzer's office, and sat down in front of his desk which was unusually tidy and had photos of him and his family smiling towards us. He had no idea why we were there, but we sat right down and got comfortable.

"Mr. Spitzer, Sandy is pregnant." I said, point blank, as she and I sat in his office. I just wanted to get it out as quickly as possible. I never saw that man's jaw drop before, but it did that afternoon. He looked panic-stricken.

"There's more. Roger is the father." His eyes almost fell out of his head. He was still and quiet. "Sandy thinks she may have been pregnant since this summer." I could see him doing the math, as I had, and I saw his big Adam's apple gyrate as he swallowed hard.

"Mrs. Preuss," he said, "Please leave Sandy and I alone for a moment."

"Sandy, I promised I'd stay with you, but Mr. Spitzer is your counselor. He might have things to say to you that he needs to say privately. Can you talk to him now and I'll wait right outside the door?"

"Yeah," she hesitated, "but stay by the door."

"I will."

After a long quiet, there was a bit of yelling going on which concerned me, but Sandy had been my student less than a month, and I really wasn't sure what had gone on before or what Mr. Spitzer actually knew, and was privy to. It was possible that Sandy was pulling my leg about the whole thing, and he already knew. I'd been warned about how 'these students' could fabricate things, but in my heart of hearts, I believed her.

When they emerged from the office, her mascara was all over her face, tracked with tears, and he, shaking his head, looking stunned and disheveled. Sure enough, we were on our way to her house to tell her foster family. On the way, I was briefed that he'd called the foster mother and said we needed to bring Sandy home and talk to her. He said he'd do the talking. I went along for the ride and to support Sandy. But, before we even got to the house, she started swearing up a storm and calling him every sort of name in the book.

She and Mr. Spitzer had a history. He'd been her counselor for years. He'd dealt with her every time she told a teacher where to stick it for the last three years. Apparently things hadn't always been smooth between them. He was a decent man, but he didn't always say what kids wanted to hear. Having never witnessed such a spectacle, I didn't know what to do. The policy in Beach County, where I'd worked before, had been very hands-off. You'd never take a kid in your car anywhere. Here I was in a new county... in a new school... in a unique program. I didn't know what to expect or whether or not this was the usual way of doing things, but I trusted Mr. Spitzer, and his insight into, and understanding of the inner workings of this at-risk population, so I kept my mouth closed, and let the two of them yell it out. "Motherf***er... A**hole... Lying Bastard!" On and on it went, and he just kept driving. "Ugly, fat-forheaded pr***, Mother f***ing lying turd, Mother f***ing Scum bag, lying sack of sh**."

She called him everything in the book. I'd never heard anything like it. We pulled up to the home, and it looked like he'd been there before and her foster mom sure knew who he was. I reached out my hand and shook hers to introduce myself, trying to put the disturbing episode in the car behind me. Before I had a chance to say much, Sandy shot out of the car and started up yelling again, and screaming more obscenities at Mr. Spitzer.

"Sandy," her foster mother screamed. "Don't you yell at him like that. You need to remember your manners!" Mrs. Clary looked embarrassed. But that didn't change much.

"I hate him!" She yelled, and ran in the house, her red and green braided hair beads bouncing noisily as she ran and slammed the door behind her.

I had no idea what the two of them had talked about in his office, but whatever it was it had unraveled her emotions. What could he have told her to make her go berserk? I didn't know, and it would be a few days before I found out. I just wanted to be there for her and for that foster mom who was about to have a big atomic bomb land in her lap.

We adults were all still standing outside the house when Sandy popped her head out the door and yelled, "Don't you dare talk to my foster mom! Don't you say one word to her. Only Ms. Preuss. Only Ms. Preuss!"

"Mrs. Clary," he started, completely ignoring her. "There's something we need to talk about."

Sandy ran outside and pushed him against the car. "I said not you!" she shrieked. He looked shocked, but brushed it off quickly. Perhaps he didn't think I was up to the task, but he was planning to start in again and give this poor woman the bad news right there on the street with Sandy crying, yelling, and pushing him around. I think she even kicked him a few times.

I knew I had to take over for her sake, as well as his. I pulled Sandy off of Mr. Spitzer and held her. I put one hand on his stomach, to let him know to stay out of it for a minute. It was all so raw and visceral and so un-educator like that I was spellbound within the humanity of the moment. I'd never been faced with such a thing. A mother/legal guardian confused, a girl in turmoil, a big buffalo of a man trying to sort through an alleged rape and a pregnancy the best he could. It was one of the wildest moments of my career. I was on a frightening rollercoaster thrill ride, trying hard to hang on!

"Sandy, shhhh, calm down. I'll do all the talking." I held her against my waist and said, "Don't worry, Sweetie." I turned to her mother, "May we go inside?"

"We don't have time to go inside, Mrs. Preuss," said Mr. Spitzer. "I'm expected to run the bus schedule after school."

I looked at my watch. The busses were due in 10 minutes. I realized that what Mr. Spitzer was telling me is that he fully intended to have this wrapped up in a few minutes and be on his way back to school to run the busses. I thought that was the most insensitive and insane thing I'd ever heard. I don't know where I got the courage to overstep him, but I had Sandy's best interest in my mind, certainly not the bus schedule's.

"No. They'll have to run them without you." He looked perplexed. He was a retired military man and schedules were very important to him. "Look at your watch. This will take a while longer than we've got." I couldn't believe I actually had to say that!

"I guess I could call 'the boss'." That's what he affectionately called the Principal.

"Yes, call the boss," I said, and left him standing out by his car, and went on in the house.

"I hate that man," Sandy said again, adding a few profane words to her sentence, as we entered, her foster mother sending a reproachful glare her way. I knew she didn't really hate him. He had always been the one who was there to help her. She was just so angry, and her life was so very out of her control, that all her anger was focused on Mr. Spitzer, and I realized, he had the profound intuition to understand that, and let it be.

She had a few choices of where to sit, but she sat right next to me on the couch in the living room of her house. Younger siblings and a baby were running around. I didn't know which were biological and which were foster kids, and I guess it didn't matter. Piles of clean laundry to be ironed were on the ironing board, and I could smell something cooking in the kitchen. It was an odd scenario for what I was about to do. I began with general conversation about how Sandy had managed in my class so far.

Mrs. Clary, looked tired and was older than I'd expected. She interrupted me with a smile. "We're so happy she's in your class! And she's happy too! She's always writing in her journals. She isn't failing is she? She hasn't been acting up again has she?" I was certain at that point that foster mom was clueless. The conversation I was about to undertake was so far beyond grades and classroom behavior, that I had to take a breath to continue.

"No problems. I love having her in my class. She's been a great addition, always quiet and attentive during instruction, and so smart."

Mrs. Clary looked so pleased by the news, I hardly had the heart to continue. It all seemed so common place to her that I began to wonder how many such confrontations Sandy and Mr. Spitzer might have had in the last year when Sandy cursed out a teacher or had a fight. How many might have ended with a teacher visit to the home in the year Sandy had lived at the Clary's? My head was already spinning with the matter at hand, so to be captured by so many thoughts and wonderings caught me off guard.

It appeared to me that Mrs. Clary was preparing for a garden variety parent-teacher conference. I knew she expected to hear something about a fight, or a theft, or that Sandy had told a teacher in the hallway where to stick it. This made my job all the more difficult. If Mrs. Clary was planning to adopt Sandy, that meant she'd be a grandmother too. I wasn't sure how she would take the news. I talked around things for a moment or two to give Mr. Spitzer enough time to finish his call, and come inside. He slipped quietly through the screen door, needing to lower his head as he entered, he was that tall. Then he sat down next to me on the couch. It was time to get to business.

"Mrs. Clary, I know you love Sandy like your own daughter, and want to formally adopt her. I can't tell you how wonderful it is to know that Sandy has you in her life. But, today something has come to my attention. Sandy wanted me to come here with her. She didn't want to tell you alone. That's why I'm here." Mr. Spitzer sat quietly. It was almost comical. The three of us were squeezed on that couch.

"Sandy," I said, "do you want to tell your mom?"

"You," Sandy said.

"Mrs. Clary, there's no easy way to say this." I paused to take a slow breath. "Sandy thinks she is pregnant." Her mother's hand came up to her mouth, and her eyes widened.

"I'm not sure why she hasn't told anyone, but she says she's suspected it since the summer." I saw her panic when she realized how far along her foster child could be. It wasn't my place to make judgments on the beliefs of others regarding abortion. It's a tough issue and one I leave to each individual to decide upon. I can't imagine what it must feel like to be faced with an unwanted pregnancy. I think unless you have walked that path it's not really something you can understand. I don't try to understand it. I just sympathize with anyone who has to look it in the face and make a decision about it.

I didn't know Mrs. Clary's beliefs, and I wasn't sure whether or not she was doing the math in her head, but it didn't matter either way. If her Sandy's suspicions were correct, she was going to be a foster grandmother in just a few months.

We had to get into the details of Sandy's story, about how Roger had forced himself on her several months before. I left out the part about them being high at the time. I don't think her foster mom believed for a moment that Roger had raped Sandy. She was neither outraged, nor threatening to call the police. She just gave Sandy a long and lasting stare. Sandy took it in, accepting it. No charges were ever pressed against him to my knowledge. But he did disappear from the school shortly thereafter.

All the crying and talking took over an hour, but by the time we left, Mrs. Clary was calm. Sandy was calm. And both of them hugged tightly as Sandy sat on the arm rest of her foster mother's chair.

"We'll have to tell dad, but not today." she said sternly.

Sandy started to cry. "Is he going to kill Roger?"

"No, Sandy, he isn't going to kill anyone." She bit her lower lip a bit, but still, I was surprised at her poise. Perhaps being a foster parent, she had been through a few of these before? I wasn't sure. Then she said something that made Sandy run over and hug her. "We are a family now, that's already been decided, so we are going to deal with this as a family."

I was happy that Sandy was able to know her mistakes hadn't put her at risk of losing the family she so desperately hoped to call her own, and I was happy to see that the issue of race never came up with us there.

Mrs. Clary learned to grasp and accept the inevitable, as we all must do from time to time. From that moment on, Roger seemed to be a non-issue, perhaps by the foster parent's choice. And that was fine with me. It seemed that Mrs. Clary was as smitten by Sandy, as Sandy was with Mrs. Clary. They held each other tightly. They did look like a real family. It's difficult to see how these kids get pushed from one home to another in foster care. Situations like Sandy's were few and far between. Mrs. Clary seemed like an old soul, with a good heart, who was genuine in her wish to provide Sandy a real home.

We said our goodbyes and Mr. Spitzer and I drove off. I felt completely numb on the way home, like I had felt so many things all at once that I had nothing left to feel. I couldn't believe what I had just experienced. I felt an awakening of sorts. Mr. Spitzer said he thought I'd missed my calling. He said I should have been a counselor. It made me wonder if maybe I should have. I was always very good at dealing with difficult issues.

Sandy came to school the next day, and told me that her foster father had taken it better than expected, only swearing just a little, and they were going to try really hard to speed up the process and formally adopt her. I was happy to hear that. They really did love Sandy, and accepted this. Now that the truth was out, I took a breath, and braced myself for what was to come!

Sandy wanted very much to stay in school and in my class. She was working hard, getting high marks, and developing relationships with the others in the class. The school, however, was suggesting the family take her out and send her to an Alternative School before she was showing. Sandy dug in her heels and refused to leave. "No! I won't go! I won't go!" She would say.

It was soon after that that Roger was withdrawn from school with little notice. I assume Mr. Spitzer or the Clary's informed his family of the situation. If Sandy was pregnant, and willing to let everyone know, then I assume his family realized it would be in his best interest to quietly 'get out of Dodge,' as the saying goes. He soon withdrew from our memories, as well. Even from Sandy's, I think. To my knowledge she never spoke his name again. Her baby was going to be, just that, *her* baby, and she had full intentions to finish school after it was born.

One day, about a week after telling her family, Sandy was late for school. When she finally got to class, she was winded, angry, and shot in the door screaming, "I hate that man!"

I took her to my little office, a room behind glass against the west wall of my classroom. I left the others to do their assignment, and closed the door behind us. Sandy explained to me that the reason she was so upset at Mr. Spitzer is because he was telling her that because she was pregnant, she should leave Destiny Middle School. That could potentially affect her placement in the Clary home. That's what he told her behind closed doors that first day. That's what had set her off to such a degree that she would yell profanities and beat a grown man in front of the foster mother who was considering adopting her.

"If you want to stay in my class it's fine with me. But if there are school rules about it, then I can't over step that. Let me make a few calls."

That afternoon I got on the phone and investigated her legal rights.

The next day when she came to school I called her in my office again, and shut the door.

"Sandy, if you refuse to go to an Alternative School, I don't think they will be able to legally *force* you to go. I think they would prefer that you leave on your own so that you can be around others in your situation, and so the kids here don't have to find out. There's a school that has a program for pregnant girls. Would you feel better being around others in the same condition as you?"

"I want to stay here, Miss," she said resolutely.

"What about the things that might be said? The things that made you so angry you were fighting with Roger? It might get worse once everyone knows you are pregnant."

She thought for a moment. I looked at her, in what may have been her last moments of childhood. She was going to be a mom very soon. "I don't care about what they say no more. I want to stay here, Miss."

"Then I'll help you do that." She looked in my eyes with trust. I wasn't going to let anyone pressure her out unless it was her decision.

I had a few talks with Mr. Spitzer, and with the Head Guidance Counselor. I let both of them know my feelings and what Sandy wanted. I called Sandy's foster mom and I told her what I'd done. I reassured her that if she wanted her daughter to come to Destiny Middle School, even when she was showing, that I would support her, Sandy, and the family, and that the school was willing to do the same.

Sandy was the first pregnant girl in anyone's memory ever to carry her baby full term while attending Destiny Middle School. As her baby belly grew, the entire class became protective of her.

As we walked to lunch all the boys would circle around her and make sure she was safe. "Watch out! Make some room!" the boys would say.

She proudly walked about the cafeteria, which was the only time she was around the general population, with her belly full blown. Occasionally, she would get comments, but she would handle them, and for the most part they were inquiries, not insults.

I think things were about as smooth as could be expected, considering the circumstances. What I noticed most was the odd hush as I walked my class to and from lunch. No one ever said anything rude to her, or offensive, that I know of.

Sandy gave me so much. The entire school learned to respect others through her. She always held her head high. She never felt sorry for herself. Everyone looked on, in quiet wonder, at the girl with the big belly in my DOP class, walking toe to toe with all the others.

The memory that most stands out is how we'd all walk in a straight line to lunch. The other students were allowed to enter the lunchroom freely when the bell rang, but my class walked in a straight line, single file, through the full cafeteria. Amid my motley crew of colorful characters of every race, disposition, and physical dimension, was Sandy, big as a barrel, beginning to waddle with a baby in her belly, but acting like any other kid in middle school, hungry and racing to get to the front of the lunch line.

For me it was a great triumph that she was able to stay in school, in my class, where she was safe and loved by me and the other students. She carried her baby till late March, and gave birth to a beautiful, baby boy with dark cappuccino colored skin and brown curls. I was in the hospital with her the day she was born. Dalia, Ashley, Latoya, Dawn and

I were all there. It was a sort of field trip we all took. All the girls had wanted to be there, but I took those who got permission from their parents. It was the first time in more than fourteen years of teaching that I had ever allowed students to be in my car. That's usually a big liability risk for an educator, but it was a risk I was willing to take.

She was so proud as she showed us her son in her arms. Her 'mom and dad' were there. There was love in that hospital room. We stayed over an hour, talking and cooing over her beautiful baby boy.

Sandy finished out the last month and a half of school from home, regularly sending in her assignments, and Mr. Spitzer and I made sure she got full credit for the year. She brought her baby in a couple of times towards the end of the year. I heard it ruffled some feathers around the school. Some folks didn't think she should come show off her baby like it was a badge of honor. I heard it being said that she was sending a bad message to the regular population. But to us it was always joyful and the entire class, even the boys, felt like they were a part of a large extended family that was growing.

She did go to regular high school that next fall, and her mom took care of the baby during the day along with all her other charges. Sandy did well in school and graduated with her class. Her dream had come true. I was sitting proudly in the audience that day. Only eleven of my students from that year made it through to graduation, but Sandy was one of them. She was lucky to have the Clary's. Every time she visited me she seemed more and more a lady than the time before, and I got to watch her baby grow into a boy as she brought him year after year to visit my incoming DOP classes.

In 2008, at the Florida League of Middle Schools Conference, where I presented a workshop about dealing with troubled youth in the classroom setting, Sandy was at my side, along with a few of the others from the early years in DOP. They had come, now grown, to support me. They had come to tell their stories. They had come to speak to a conference room filled with teachers about how to cope with kids like themselves.

What pride I felt to have five of my former students there, presenting along side of me. Mrs. Clary sat in the back row with Sandy's son, who behaved formidably, and seemed very proud of his mother on the stage. My own children were there, managing the camera, and microphone. It seemed like a wonderful pinnacle to have reached with my DOP students, to now be sharing to other teachers with them, along side of my own two sons!

* * *

Sandy still calls me from time to time, and sends me pictures on Facebook. Her boy is in school now and she is a nursing student, working at Beach Haven Memorial. Through her struggles, she taught me many lessons about life, and how people learn to interact with one another, mold themselves as needed, learn to think beyond the realm of their own possibilities. I will always be indebted to her for exposing me in a very real way to the realities of young life for kids who sit in classrooms across America. She took a pivotal role in my life because of this, and in the lives of many of the other girls in my class that year. In fact, she became an unlikely and unforgettable example to the entire school, children and adults alike, of a significant young person of courage, character, and unyielding will.

SANDY'S JOURNAL

Being pregnant and coming to school is not easy. I have to learn to just think about my goal, and not my mistakes. I made a lot of mistakes, but now I want to make my goals.

* * *

CHAPTER NINE

DALIA

On the way back from visiting Sandy at the hospital, I dropped all the girls off. Ashley, Dawn and Dalia all lived on the same main highway. I had never been to their homes, but I knew they lived in apartments that were small, from what they told me, and what I read in their journals. When I went to drop off Dalia, the last of the three girls, I stopped my car where she asked. It wasn't an apartment. It was a motel.

"Will you wait outside for a minute and make sure I can get in?" she asked.

I thought it was odd that she couldn't get in on her own, so I asked, "Why wouldn't you be able to get in?"

"My mom has a new boyfriend and she gave him my key."

"Okay, Dalia, I'll be right here." I waited by the side of the road and watched her inch up to the yellow door of the blue motel with the flashing sign, Breezeway Inn. It may have been the longest few minutes of my life. I knew that many of our students were from low economic homes. Destiny is a Title I School. That means that a high percentage of the school students are receiving free and reduced lunch. Because of it we get special funding. I knew to expect poverty in many cases, but never in my wildest dreams did I expect to find Dalia, beautiful Dalia, well-dressed, always sharp, neatly ironed Dalia to be living in a motel room.

I thought of my own children, who were probably then playing in the backyard of my home, being watched by the loving eyes of their grandmother. I knew that even when I was away from home, like that day, my children were cared for. My mother was never far from their side when I wasn't home. I imagined them playing on the swing, and eating sandwiches and drinking milk. I imagined them doing their homework. I imagined so many things that Dalia wasn't experiencing in her little hotel room. This was her home, nevertheless.

I watched her knock on the door, then yell through the window. I watched and wondered how she was able to come to school each day, homework completed, clothes tidy, make-up on and looking so good. I knew her mother didn't speak English. I had spoken to her a few times in Spanish over the phone, and I met her at school for Parent Night. She was a lovely and well-spoken woman who had left her native Panama when her husband began beating the children. Dalia had an older brother who still lived in Panama with his grandmother. This much I knew.

Dalia was a nice girl, but I think her mother was out of touch with the realities of the United States of America. Most specifically, the city of Beach Haven, Florida. She would often leave Dalia with neighbors, whom Dalia said she got drugs from. Right between the two main streets in Beach Haven, no more than half a mile apart, there is a drug corridor that runs north and south for many miles, and through several counties. I never knew anything about it until I started teaching at Destiny. In fact, I lived within the corridor for many years and didn't even know it was a corridor.

"You don't see the drugs, Miss, cuz you ain't looking for them," Dalia would tell me. "They are everywhere."

Dalia often came to school red-eyed and still high from the night before. She would hold it together the best she could in class. When it first started, I told Mr. Spitzer about it. "What are you going to do, Mrs. Preuss? Send her home so she can get high again? Just keep her in your class unless she acts up. She won't do anyone any good on the streets. And chances are she'd have to walk home or take the bus in that condition."

"How can you say that, Mr. Spitzer? Her mother should know."

"Her mother knows, but she can't stop her. Trust me, Mrs, Preuss. Your class is the best thing she has going."

When I first had that discussion with him, earlier in the year, long before Sandy had come along, I had thought him a bit a bit unprofessional, and his tactics risky. Over time, I came to see quite clearly, how he knew more about my students' lives and ways than I did. My sitting outside this motel would be one example of that. *He was right. School was the best thing she had going.* My realization of that would prove to be mind shattering.

Dalia came to the car a minute and said, "Can you wait a little more? I can ask the manager to open it, if he's there."

"Sure, go ahead." I said, wondering how my own life would have been different if I'd ever had to run around a roadside motel looking for a manager to open my motel room door because my mother had given her boyfriend the key I should have had. It perplexed me how stupid I had been as a teacher all the years before now. I remembered all the times I had yelled at a student who had forgotten homework. It never occurred to me, that in a small hotel room, it might have gotten lost. It never occurred to me that in a small hotel room where a mother and daughter and a random boyfriend all lived together, homework might not have been the first thing done when a student got 'home from school.' And it certainly never occurred to me that a student might not even be able to get inside their own home to safety when they needed.

As I waited there, I realized how ridiculous the concept of homework was for some kids. My hands held the steering wheel, and I almost began to weep. My heart pounded, as I watched her go from door to door, upstairs and down. How many of my students lived like this? Do teachers even understand as they drive to their suburban homes, what a student of poverty goes through?

Those few minutes opened my eyes forever. I never again got angered over missing homework, which sometimes I tended to take personally. In my ignorance of how these kids function, I thought it was simply disrespectful not to bring in a homework assignment, especially a simple one. I used to get really heated at times, yelling at entire classes when a large percentage of kids had forgotten their homework. How ridiculous it all seemed to me as I sat parked in front of The Breezeway Inn.

She was on her way back to the car, and I thought the worst was over, but it wasn't. The worst was about to present itself.

She hunched over the car, and poked her pretty face in. Her black eyes that were streaked with brown were among the brightest, biggest and most beautiful I'd ever seen. She had long eyelashes that were always curled high in mascara, and a thick black liner edged them on both sides. Usually she wore blue eyeshadow, the kind you have to brush on wet and thick. Her dark brown hair went to her waist, and she often wore it in a simple pony tail. She wore her clothes tight to show off her curves, and often wore sandal heels to school, which made her look a bit older than her 14 years. I smelled her soft perfume through my window. Her face looked tense.

"What's the matter, Sweetie?" I asked.

"The manager isn't there, and nobody has seen my mom or her boyfriend today. One lady said she had a fight with him last night, and nobody has seen her since."

I was stunned about her predicament. Of course I worried about her mother, but I was more worried about Dalia and where she had slept. I didn't want to give that away, so I played it off as best I could. "Grown-ups argue. I'm sure she's fine. Do you have a place to call her?"

"She got a new job at a different restaurant, and I don't know it." This was still a time when kids didn't all have cell phones, and certainly didn't bring them to school with regularity. I had gotten permission a few days before to take her to the hospital, so perhaps the mother had forgotten she would come home later. I felt responsible.

"I hope my getting you home late isn't the reason you can't get in," I said, concerned.

"Naw, Miss, don't worry, she's almost never home when I get home. It's just that she gave the key. That's all. If I can't get in she lets me stay with a neighbor, but that b**ch is a crack head, and she ain't home anyway."

I looked at her softly, never letting my face show her the thoughts that raced through my head. *How could a mother give her daughter's key away to a boyfriend?* I wanted to take her to my house and take care of her. I wanted to give her a warm meal. I wanted to make her feel safe and tuck her in to a bed in a bedroom that had pink curtains and a name plaque over a desk saying, "Dalia." I was furious at how she existed. I was furious at the circumstances that had brought her mother to a foreign country, to a crack corridor, to a cheap motel. I was furious that she had to work three jobs and couldn't keep an eye on Dalia. I was furious that she trusted a crackhead because she didn't know a crackhead when she saw one. I was furious about so many things.

"Just take me to my boyfriend's house. I can get in there. He leaves the window open for me."

"Dalia, I can't let you crawl into a window."

"Sure you can. I do it all the time."

"And your mother knows?"

"Of course she knows. She likes Miguel a lot."

"Dalia, did you sleep at Miguel's last night?"

"Yeah," she said, as if she replied to a question about breakfast cereals. "I sleep with him the nights my mom has to work."

I knew her mom worked all night cleaning, and at a restaurant during the day, and had a job at the flea market every other weekend. I knew Dalia had a boyfriend who was a few years older than her. I knew Dalia was sexually active. I knew she had little supervision at home. I knew her mother was overwhelmed and couldn't handle her daughter. I knew Dalia had a history of drug use. I knew all those things. So why was I so shocked as I spoke to her in my car?

It's interesting how within the context of a classroom things look different. As the scene unfolded before me, I understood more than I wanted to understand about this little girl's life. I imagined her coming home from school to an empty hotel room and crawling into a window to wait for her boyfriend, and do drugs. I was surprised she came to school at all.

"So that's quite a few nights."

"Okay, Miss. I pretty much stay at both places. He takes care of stuff for us, and gives us money sometimes. My mom likes him. We even lived with him for a while last year. It's okay. You don't have to worry."

For a moment I thought about driving her over to the police station and reporting this to the authorities. Thoughts of my other student, Ashley, who I witnessed being dragged into a police car in shackles one afternoon at school, knocked me to my senses. I knew better than to call HRS into anything before really thinking it through. I knew handcuffs and shackles would be in her future if I did. I imagined Dalia spending the night in a cold jail cell. *I would drive her to Miguel's house.*

I felt as if I was in a movie, as I drove the few blocks to Miguel's house. If this was Dalia's life, this was Dalia's life. If her mother allowed her fourteen year old to sleep with her boyfriend, who was I to get in the way of that? I had to tell myself it was none of my business.

I drove around to the boyfriend's house and by now a light rain had begun. "I'll wait here till you come back and tell me you got in and you are safe." I watched her knock on the door to no avail. Then I saw her go around the back of his duplex apartment, presumably, to go through the window.

It was as if a brick had landed on my head and my brain splattered everywhere. I couldn't believe what I was doing. *Should I drive her to the police station after all?* My heart raced as fast as my thoughts. A few minutes later, she came bouncing out of the door with a smile and came to my car.

"He was sleeping, Miss. Do you want to meet him?"

"No, Dalia. I have to get going, Sweetie." It had been rumored through other kids that the boyfriend she was seeing was in a gang, and dealt drugs. I never believed anything they said, because they said so many unimaginable things that if I believed them all, half of them would be in foster homes, and the other half arrested. My policy was to think of every story as fantasy fiction until I thought a child was in danger, or they specifically asked me for help.

Was Dalia in enough imminent danger to put her through what Ashley had gone through? She was indoors, out of the rain. She was with someone her mother trusted. I thought it best for Dalia not to bring in any authorities. It's a decision that haunts me to this day.

I waved goodbye, and left her there in front of his duplex. I looked back, and she was going inside with a happy skip in her step. I don't even remember driving home, but when I got there, I hugged my children tightly. I hugged my mother who was at my home watching them, while I was delayed. And two hours later, I hugged my husband and cried in his arms as I told him the story.

I took a long shower, letting the water pound on me. I wondered if I'd done the right thing. I wept for a long time in the shower, and with the tears went my innocence as an educator. I would never again think I knew anything about anything. I realized I knew nothing at all.

I didn't sleep all night, paced some, sat with my head held between my hands. Thoughts of Dalia climbing into windows raced over and over again in my mind. And in the morning, I couldn't wait to get to school to see Dalia. To make sure, I'd done the right thing. She showed up bright and early, and brought in her homework. She sat in her chair like she did every day, listening and doing all her assignments. Her eyes were clear and bright.

I called her into my little office, as the kids wrote in their journals as they did each morning. I had so many questions for her, and she answered them all.

Her mother was fine, and had gone to work last night. Dalia had seen her that morning.

"She broke up with that boyfriend is all, Miss. And it's a good thing, cuz he always smelled like beer."

"Yeah. Beer stinks, doesn't it?" We both laughed a little.

"She wasn't worried since I was with you."

"I'm glad, but I still want to call her today."

"Sure. Go ahead. She'll tell you it was okay to go to Miguel's."

"Does Miguel live alone?"

"Sometimes, but not all the time."

"What do you mean, Dalia?"

"It's a long story, Miss."

"Do you want to write me all about it in your journal today?

She smiled and said yes.

DALIA'S JOURNAL

My boyfriend name is Miguel Diego. He is real cute. He got me a ring with a diamond. I knowed him since I was 10 years old when I came from my country. He's four years older than me. When I leave Panama, he with me all the time in the apartment next to where I live with my mom and my bother. He taught me English a lot, and he was friends with my brother. Then my brother went to Panama to live with my grandmother. Then when we get kicked out of our apartment, he help my mom and me, and we even live with him for 5 months, with him and his uncle. His uncle's in gangs and he's in gang too, but not so much. His uncle sometimes leaves and then he alone for a while. We going to get married when I am 18. I never been with nobody else. I know you maybe think it wrong, but he love me a lot and he the one for me. Please don't tell my mom he in a gang. That the only thing she don't know for sure.

My mom lives with me here in Florida now. It different here than in Panama. In Panama my whole family live. Here, we alone. I hate it here. Only good thing is I see my boyfriend, Miguel, and I learn English.

* * *

Later in the day, I spoke to Dalia's mother. She seemed unfazed by the events of the previous night, and thanked me profusely for driving her daughter and apologized for not being home.

Dalia married Miguel a few years after she left my class, and they had two kids. I visited her a few times after each baby was born. I only saw Miguel once. He was sitting in a big car, and had tattoos on his arm. He came out of the car and shook my hand. He wore baggy pants that came half way down his butt, and a loose fitting shirt. We locked eyes briefly.

After that Dalia and I talked several times a year for a while. I'll never forget one year, she called and said she had moved to California.

"Miguel is a lieutenant now," she said.

I was so proud. I figured he had gotten into the armed forces and cleaned up his act. "Wow," I said. "A lieutenant! You can be very proud of him. Is he in the army?"

She had a big laugh over that one. "Naw, Ms. Preuss, he's a lieutenant with the famous XYZ Gang of L.A."

I swallowed hard. "What about the babies? Are they okay?" I tried to keep talking while this whole famous XYZ Ganf of L.A, thing sank in.

"Yeah, they're with my mom all day. She lives with us."

"Please tell your mom I said hello." The idea that Dalia's mother, the well-spoken, neatly dressed woman who came from Panama for a better life was living in L.A. in the home of a high level XYZ gang member, was astounding. But I held my tongue.

"Is everybody treating you good, Ms. Preuss? Because if not, you just tell me and I can have them smoked."

In some oddly profound way, I was honored that she was willing to go that far for me, as to put have a bullet put into someone if I asked. That's something no one ever offered me before.

"I hope you're kidding, Dalia."

"No mam. You just say the word and I will smoke anybody who messes with you."

"You are not smoking people yourself are you?"

She laughed. "No. But Miguel's homeboys can smoke them for you."

I was amazed at how I could love her so much, and hate what she was doing. I seemed to be able to keep my feelings for her separate from my feelings about her choices. It's something I've had to learn how to do over the years.

Miguel went in and out of gang activity until he was finally arrested after a drive by shooting that resulted in several deaths. He would be behind bars for the rest of his life.

The last time I spoke to Dalia, she said she was done crying for Miguel, and had tired of the gang life. She had moved in with a nice man who sold cars for a living. I was so relieved, and happy to hear that.

We talked about her family and the kids. A third baby was on the way and she seemed so happy. Her life was coming together so nicely.

"I got my GED, Miss. And after I have the baby, I'm going to go to classes to be an X ray technician."

"That's wonderful. I'm so proud of you," I said. She sounded so grown up. I felt happy to know she was carving a good path for herself after everything she'd been through.

"I had to write an essay to get into the X ray school. I did it just like you said, with all the paragraphs organized and supporting the topic sentences. I had to say why it was important for me to go to school. I explained about my life before, Miss. I told them how it was, like I did in my journals. They really liked it. I write so much better in English now. That's because of you. You made me feel like I could write even when I couldn't."

"You could always write, Dalia, I always knew what you wanted to say."

"I read a lot too, Miss, like you told me to do. You know that book, Thorn Birds, you like so much? I've read it five times. It's a great story. I really get it now, how the little bird in the poem at the front of the book doesn't know any better, and it looks for a thorn to die on while it sings its best song. I'm the bird, right Miss?"

My heart stopped, and every scene I'd lived with her when she was just fourteen flashed inside my head. In an instant, Dalia had opened forevermore my once-closed educators' eyes, and cleared me of the narrow-minded arrogance and ignorance with which I once conducted my practice. Because of her, and those like her, I saw life and people in new, unfiltered, authentic, and unexpected ways.

Because of her, and all the rest, I learned never to judge others. Because of her, I was freed of a lifetime of conditioned responses and learned "shoulds" and "shouldn'ts." I was liberated of the ties that bind some educators' hands behind their backs, and their minds in the 20th century, making them mere caricatures of themselves. Because of her, and all of them, I am more human and more humane.

Because of all of them, I am awakened!

It didn't matter how I tried to tell her, she would never understand how she had been *my* teacher, and given me much more than I had given her.

Yes, Dalia, the bird who sings while dying on a thorn is all of us! I was just happy she couldn't see my tears.

CHAPTER 10

VOICES IN THE HALL

What I've put together here is merely the tip of the iceberg. I started this book so very long ago, and for fear that I will once again retreat, put it in a drawer and say, it's not good enough, I put it out there, now. As it is.

These stories, living in my heart for a decade, beg to be told. I can no longer pretend that this book is about me. I can no longer ask: Is it ready? Will I ever finish? Where will I find the time? Who is my audience? These questions fall into a stream of fast moving water, never to be answered.

It's about the kids. This is theirs. It doesn't matter if it's good or bad. It doesn't matter if you like it or not. It's about the kids. This is who they are and this is who they were to me.

Recently, thanks to an incredible invention called Facebook, I've gotten in touch with many of my former students. They are writers, singers, nurses, office clerks, roofers, teachers, law enforcement officers, gang members, mothers, dads, and yes, some are behind bars. They still reach out to me and each other. They still wonder why I haven't published my book: their stories.

I have trouble reconciling why it's taken so long. I wrote it a decade ago, just after 9/11. I sent it out and got wonderful rejection letters. Most had hand-written statements from editors and publishers, encouraging me on. I even got a rejection phone call. It was that powerful, that a publisher actually called me to explain why he had to say no!

We had a chat about 'my audience.' Who is my audience?

At first I wrote this book for adults. Dear World… This is what you need to know about kids today. That was my concept, but there was too much profanity, too much sensitive material, they said. So I put it in a drawer, where it collected dust until one day, I took it out to see what kids thought about it.

I realize now, the kids were always my audience, but I didn't know it. Reading it today, editing out some of the more disturbing parts, bleeping out the cuss words I couldn't take out, changing and tweaking it so kids can read it - so I can bring it out in a classroom and actually use it, without needing to worry it isn't "kid-friendly" enough, makes me realize, there are parts in it that aren't written to kids, and parts that aren't written to adults. Because… this book is for everyone. This book does not want to be confined to a pre determined "audience."

It's for the world. Just the way we started, when I would have the kids write in their journals, and I would say, "Imagine you are telling the world what they need to know about you. Dear World… This book is for whoever wants to read it. It contains stories inspired by real kids and real events, but they are stories, think of them as fictional if you must, as I had to at times. Names and places are changed. Events and characters are blended to maintain anonymity and deniability. They can come forward and introduce themselves and their own stories to the world one by one, from wherever they are. That's their right if they want to do so. But, I will never disclose who is who and what is what.

Some of it is directed to parents and educators, but the stories are the kid's own. Their lives, relatable by other kids. That may surprise some of the adults. But in every school in America you have your Kyles, and your Ashleys, and your Dawns and your Dalias and your Rafes and your Chungos and they are sitting in classrooms, wanting to be heard. They come from worlds their teachers or the school system may not understand, but they are there, and their hearts are good. Always, their hearts are good. I've never found that to be different.

I look into the heart and find the best in each kid. I find something to love in each and every one. Sometimes it's hard, because they often put up a wall and act like they don't want you to love them, but if you search, it's there. That something lovable in each one, *is* there! My job as an educator has been to find that thing to love, hard as it may be, dig as I must. I always find the bright sparkle in each student--at least I have since meeting the cast of characters described here in August of 2000.

Since that first year, other DOP classes have followed in much the same suit. The people, the personalities, and the stories differed, but the aim, the purpose, and the outcome remained the same. In each class, year after year, we became a close family and I continued to connect with each class that followed through honest acceptance, unconditional love and non-judgmental communication. Through their words and their writing, the same method that unfolded that first year, unfolded every year after. I continued to find my experiences with this distinct student population fascinating, inspiring, challenging, compelling, rewarding, and wonderful, and I have been able to take what I learned to all my students, in every type of class I've taught since then.

Each class, each child, has connected me even further with the universal voice of today's troubled youth. They join the thousands of voices that have touched me in such profound ways that their stories have woven themselves into the fabric of my being. I can never again disconnect myself from the problems they are facing as I attempt to teach them, or from the collective consciousness they allowed me to tap into. Nor can I turn a blind eye to the responsibility of bringing other educators an awareness of who they are and how they live.

I have come to understand that the problems they face as a community of youth are the very reason it's difficult to teach so many of them. But they come. They are here and they need us to understand them.

I recognized, thanks to all of them, that if I am going to teach, I can't ignore how they live, or the struggles they face in their young lives, day in and day out. I can't pretend to believe that most educators have a clue to the issues that bubble beneath their exteriors. Most teachers have no idea what they are dealing with when their class fills with 30 kids, and they walk to their blackboards to begin teaching.

Even over the last few years, since I went back to teaching regular classes, I understood that I was formidably changed by what my DOP students had taught me. I understood when a student had a behavior problem or just didn't care about his grade, that the problem could stem from deeper roots than a traditional classroom can address with integrity and respect for what the child is living through.

I became an advocate for the troubled student. I understood things other teachers, who had never had my experience, could not understand. I have butted heads with educators over and over again in defense of the plight of our troubled, at-risk kids. There is much to uncover about the complexity of their troubled existence and how that affects learning, effort, ability, interest, and grades.

I was so drawn to helping the troubled students that eventually I requested to return to my passion. I ran an Internal Suspension program for my county at a local YMCA, and two years later I ran an Internal Suspension program at my same school. It wasn't DOP, but I impacted hundreds more students each year, and they impacted me.

Every child who got in trouble because of behavior at my county and later at my school, came to me for 1 to 10 days. In those days, I managed to keep them working quietly on their assignments while they were in a virtual detention center. I also made sure I showed them compassion, and let them know someone truly cared about them and genuinely liked them. I showed them LOVE.

Even while I made them do their schoolwork, I showed them LOVE. Even while I kept them hidden away from the general population, I showed them LOVE. Even while I provided a district-wide mandated punishment, I showed them LOVE. Even while I lectured them on the benefits of good behavior in school, I showed them LOVE. Even while I commented on the outrageous episodes of silly to dangerous acts that sometimes transpired in their school lives, I showed them LOVE. Even when I took their electronic devices, their beloved phones, and iPods, I showed them LOVE. Through this method, I was able to earn their respect in just a few days during their stint in Internal Suspension.

The reason I know how to show them LOVE is because my DOP students taught me how to LOVE even the most difficult, troubled, volatile, and dangerous kids. They taught me to find the good in each of them. They showed me their hearts.

Finding the right way to reach the world's most difficult students is an odd, yet magical balancing act that I feel I do better than most. In many ways, I feel that I have found my purpose in life. I help the kids who struggle and are misunderstood. They know that I can look them in the eye, see their faults, accept them and LOVE them just the same.

During my Internal Suspension years, I loved to see kids doing their schoolwork and behaving, even if it was just for the few days they were with me. My purpose was to give students the space and opportunity to do work for their teachers, so they could get credit while at school, rather than be suspended at home, and miss their educational time.

They did it willingly for me because they knew I genuinely cared about them, and I didn't judge them for their faults and their attitudes. Instead, thanks to my first DOP class, and those that followed, I've learned how to use their faults and their attitudes to help them see the best in themselves, which always lies just beyond their faults and attitudes.

I'm often surprised at how close I can become to kids in a short period of time. In a few days I get them, and they get me, and we are able to influence each other very quickly. It's as if we speak the same language, and because of that I can touch them in ways others can't.

For the education that my DOP students gave me, I am eternally thankful. I can never look at a child who is difficult or failing in quite the same way. I now know to search for a reason why this is so. The reason leads me to the answer… the method I need to reach that child in the way he or she needs to be reached. As an educator these students have transformed me, I loved, and they loved me right back. Today, I use the insight they brought me to reach the hearts of even the most unreachable students. I'm humbled and honored that I got to work with what schools consider "difficult" kids.

I have gone on to use their lives as examples for others.

It began during Internal Suspension. I had a number repeat offenders, or "Frequent Flyers" as I liked to call them, who kept coming back to the YMCA where I was at the time, running the county Suspension and Detention Hall. Most of them were high school students.

Parents didn't tend to send their elementary or middle school child to a county internal suspension program, so most of the kids who came were 14 to 18 years old. One day I was talking to Eric, one of my favorite Frequent Flyers, an exceptionally bright senior who was planning to get a real estate license. I told him I was a realtor in addition to being a teacher, and that piqued his interest in me enough to engage in a conversation at lunch, which was brought in for us daily from a nearby school. I also told him about this book.

"What do you mean it's in a drawer? No one has read it? It sounds interesting. Bring it in for me tomorrow."

I figured, why not. He's a senior. He can handle it.

The next day, I brought it in. I gave him a warning about the language, and he said they read stuff like that in school all the time, so I didn't worry. I told him how I'd almost gotten it published. He read it in one sitting before lunch. "Where's the rest?" he asked.

"I never finished it."

"Why not?"

"Well, if you must know, Oprah didn't return my calls!" I said, only half kidding. I actually had sent it to her as a class project, shortly after 9/1, but her people weren't accepting mail at that time due to the postal bomb threats.

He laughed, "Well, I think it's good, kids at my school would love to read this."

"Really?" I asked.

"Really! Wake up Big G and you'll see," he said, pointing over to the gigantic boy, snoring in the corner.

Big G was my *most* "Frequent Flyer," of all the "Frequent Flyers." I'm sure I saw him more than his own teachers did. He would always come in for a 10-day stint, never any less. He'd go back to class for a few days, then they'd send him right back. He was a three hundred pound defensive-end football player, and by the looks of things he must have been very good or they would have expelled him after a few suspensions.

Big G was funny. If he was awake, he was always trying to make a joke. He was the only student allowed to sleep in internal suspension. It was hard to manage that one. I knew he did drugs, and ran with a dangerous crowd; so sending him home would have been a green light for him to get into mischief. The three of us who ran the internal suspension program collectively decided that he was the one kid who we would let sleep. We'd just look the other way until he started snoring, then we'd have to make him wake up and try to get him to do his work.

This ruling had been grandfathered in. Big G had been a frequent flyer for two years before I ever got there. The previous internal suspension director had let him sleep, so I was informed of the situation the first time he came in. He'd just sort of come in early, and always on time, start to read, then fall asleep. I was sure I could make him stay awake, so I would go over to him, and tickle his arm and motion to him to lift his head, but that never lasted long. He'd smile, pick up his pencil, work for an hour or so, and then fall asleep.

After his fourth or fifth stint in internal suspension, I decided I'd sit with him and help him work. That's when I realized that he was on about a 3rd grade reading level. It didn't matter what we gave him to do, he couldn't understand it, so he would get bored, and fall asleep. I tried so many things to motivate him, but the work he was supposed to do, the work his teachers gave him, he just wasn't capable of doing.

I looked over at Big G, with his fat hands, and Flintstone feet, nappy hair with a pencil stuck in it sideways, sleeping in the corner. "Really? You think Big G will like it?"

"Yeah, Miss. Let him read it. He probably knows some of these people in your book."

I was captivated by the idea. I looked at Big G, saliva dripping down his chin and on the desk, eyes fluttering about. He must have been in deep REM phase. I looked at him, like so many other times, wondering what I could do to reach him, then it hit me, like a bolt of lightning. This book is for him.

Big G already knew I taught DOP at Destiny Middle School, and as a matter of fact, he did know some of my students. Not from the first year, but from a few years after. I did wake him up. I went over and tickled his arm, like I always did, and handed him a Kleenex to wipe off his saliva and his desk, and I signaled him to get back to his work. He smiled, and lifted his head and took the pencil from his fuzzy Afro hair and started back up on his math. Two minutes later, he was raising his hand to go to the bathroom.

I let him go on the condition he would stay awake and do his work when he came back. "Yes Miss, I promise." He didn't believe that promise anymore than I did, but I had a plan in the works and he was playing right into it.

When he came dragging back in, he sat down, and fixed his arms to lay his head back on. "Oh! No you don't. Keep your head up."

"Miss, I'm tired. I didn't get no sleep last night."

"I'm sorry to hear that, but a deal is a deal. You promised you'd go right back to your work."

"Miss, please! That junk is boring and I'm tired." He looked so sad and pathetic. His eyes traveled to the other two teachers in the room for sympathy, as usual. I wondered what drugs he had done the night before, to get him into this state.

"G," I said, rifling through his notebook, "don't you have any work in here you can do for your teachers?"

"I'll do your work. Give me some math."

I always had extra work and books from all levels and all subjects with me at the YMCA, so I grabbed some math handouts and gave them to him. It was easier than what he got from his teachers, so he could manage it alone. He knew the work we gave him was usually non-threatening. He was supposed to bring his own books and work from school, but Big G never did. So he often did multiplication and division handouts, or basic reading and writing handouts, for which we gave him a percentage grade, incorporating the amount of work, along with behavior for the day.

He thanked me and started working on the math sheets. Twenty minutes later, he made his first attempt to rest his head. "G!" I growled... "Do your work."

"Okay, okay, Miss!" He smiled and started at it again.

Another ten minutes went by when he started scratching his head, and raised his hand again.

"Miss, I finished the multiplication, but I'm tired of doing math." That was my chance!

"Here, read this," I said, placing chapter two on his desk, the one called Kyle. I had taken it out of the rest of the manuscript after Eric had read it and stapled it together like the little packets of reading I handed out when someone wanted extra reading work.

"I don't want to read, Miss. Let me just rest, I'll do my work a little later. I think I'm sick. I need to put my head down."

Maybe he *was* sick. He didn't look very good, but then again, he never really looked all that well. I mean, if he wasn't actually on the football field, he was usually getting wasted. "You'll like this story," I said, "It's a true story about a kid who gets caught with marijuana in my classroom." His eyes perked up. "I wrote it myself."

"This Kyle is one of your DOP kids?"

"Well, his real name wasn't Kyle, but yes, he was one of my students."

"What was his real name?"

"Tommy." I made up another name to protect Kyle's true identity.

"And you found marijuana on him?" Big G asked in amazement.

"Yes."

"At Destiny?!"

"That's right."

"Did he get arrested?"

"You'll have to read the story to find out." I smiled, and he smiled, I think he knew I had just *tricked* him into reading. He opened it up and started reading.

Kyle's Chapter is almost 30 pages long, and he read them through without one stop. The whole time his eyes were wide, as they searched the page, thoroughly engaged in the story in a way I'd never seen him be engaged in any learning activity.

He asked me what a few of the words meant, "What is demonic?" Minutes later, "What is stoic?" He was actually reading. Eric and I gave each other a high five.

"I told you he'd like it," Eric said.

And that's how it began. As soon as he finished he said, "That was good, Miss. You got any more of them stories?" My heart leapt, I was so happy. Eric was a smart kid who liked reading, so his interest in my work and appreciation of it was very important, but to see Big G actually enjoy reading and wanting more, and not wanting to sleep right after... well that was a great triumph for me.

"Yeah. I have, 'Chungo' about a guy who was in gangs, which he actually wrote himself, or 'Ashley' about a girl who got dragged out of school by the police in handcuffs and shackles because HRS was looking for her. Take your pick."

"The one about gangs!" He said, and excitedly handed me "Kyle" and waited by my desk for me to give him the "Chungo" chapter. He sat right down and started reading. I was impressed.

Another student from across the room who'd been watching said, "Can I read that story Big G read?"

"Of course you can, come here, I'll give it to you."

Then one of the girls asked, "Can I read the one about the girl, Miss?"

"Sure!" I said, and gave her the chapter about Ashley.

My book had become an instant hit. I have those first kids in Internal Suspension at the YMCA in Hollywood, Florida to thank for that. After that day, I made copies of the first three main chapters and stapled them into packs.

For years after that, I used these packs for Internal Suspension. It became a rite of passage. If you had been in I.S. (Internal Suspension) for a long time and behaved, you got to read one of my stories. The kids seemed impressed that I actually knew those kids, and I always made them read the newspaper article that went with it first. I found that for reluctant readers, it was very useful, especially kids who live those kinds of lives. They identify with the stories and are compelled to read it because it reaches them.

I loved hearing them talk to each other about it. Asking who had read "Kyle," and who had read "Ashley," and who had read "Chungo," and some days they would swap them amongst themselves. Those were the only three chapters I ever had in class. My DOP students had reached celebrity status. They were a living legend among the troubled kids in Suspension Hall.

Later, when I taught Language Arts and Teen Health, I would use the newspaper articles and the stories as a precursor to my journaling lessons. I felt it was important for kids to know that their stories are relevant, that others can learn from them, and that they can have a voice in society, and make a difference, and influence the world and the future, just by sharing and writing.

I had a lot of kids write me their stories and ask me to put it in my book. I felt so proud and honored. I had done something significant. Then it hit me. This is a book *by kids* and *for kids*!

It's funny how you can be so educated and the simplest things escape you. The book I had written for parents and educators was being loved and read by kids, and those kids kept telling me I had to finish the book so they could read it in school. What an inspiration my students have been to me. They have not let me retreat. They have inspired me to do this work because they need to hear these stories. Even kids who hate reading, or kids with low-level skills, want to read when they are reading about other kids' lives.

Now, more than a decade after my first DOP class, I am teaching the brightest and highest achieving kids at my school. They are great writers, and they love to read the stories too. So I know that through the accounts of so many of my students' troubles, I'm continuing to change lives and influence the future.

As the teaching profession changes with the times, I hope always to be on the cutting edge of education. I hope always to be ready for the changes the new generation needs. I hope always to teach with heart, and I know I will love every child that crosses my path, no matter what their circumstance.

I want LOVE to no longer be a four-letter word in education. I want teachers to LOVE. I want them to LOVE their jobs and the work they do. I want them to LOVE their students. I want them to find something to LOVE about each and every child. If you can just do that, they will LOVE you right back. It's like magic. Really!

I have done seminars and presentations about these kids and with these kids. I stay connected with them. I am even writing to some of them, now in jail. And I have recently started a movement called ABC+LOVE. ABC = It's About Brotherhood and Compassion + LOVE = Looking in Ourselves Visioning Excellence in Education.

My efforts now are to share as much as I can about these kids who changed me forever. I think they will come to change the world.

I know I will always listen with caring, compassion and love to the Voices in the Hall. And I hope other teachers, educators, counselors, principals and parents will learn to do the same.

Can you hear them?

Made in the USA
Middletown, DE
19 June 2017